Real Estate Partnerships

REAL ESTATE PARTNERSHIPS

How to Access More Cash, Acquire Bigger Deals, and Achieve Higher Profits

Tony J. Robinson and Ashley Kehr

BiggerPockets®
PUBLISHING
Denver, Colorado

Praise for
REAL ESTATE PARTNERSHIPS

There is no such thing as self-made success. All successful people made it with the help of their support team, whether it's family, employees, coaches, advisors, or business partners. While we each may have unique talents, we're also devoid of certain skills that are necessary to achieve our goals. This is why the wealthiest of people have mastered the art of partnership, enrolling others to share and contribute to their vision. In this book, Tony and Ashley lay out the critical steps to forming and fostering powerful partnerships both personally and professionally.

—Kathy Fettke, CEO and cofounder of the
Real Wealth Network, author of *Retire Rich with Rentals*,
and cohost of the BiggerPockets *On the Market* podcast

Henry Ford once said that "Coming together is a beginning, staying together is progress, and working together is success." Tony and Ashley's book captures all of the steps it takes to have a winning partnership. From finding the perfect partner, to establishing a solid working relationship, to even ending a partnership appropriately, there is no aspect of partnerships that is not discussed in this book. If you are looking for a partner or need to know how to strengthen your existing partnership, look no further: *Real Estate Partnerships* is the answer!

—Ashley Wilson, cofounder of Bar Down Investments and
HouseItLook, and author of *The Only Woman in the Room*

The secret to my portfolio of 10,000+ rental units? Partnerships. They've fueled 99 percent of the properties I've bought, and *Real Estate Partnerships* by Tony Robinson and Ashley Kehr will help you use partnerships to fuel your real estate growth too. This is the book I wish I had when starting out, and it's the book you need if you want to achieve significant returns in real estate investing.

—Brandon Turner, author of *The Book on Rental Property Investing* and founder of Open Door Capital and The BetterLife Tribe

Real Estate Partnerships: How to Access More Cash, Acquire Bigger Deals, and Achieve Higher Profits
Tony J. Robinson and Ashley Kehr

Published by BiggerPockets Publishing LLC, Denver, CO
Copyright © 2023 by Tony Robinson and Ashley Kehr
All rights reserved.

Publisher's Cataloging-in-Publication data
Names: Kehr, Ashley, author. | Robinson, Tony J., author.
Title: Real estate partnerships: how to access more cash , acquire bigger deals , and achieve higher profits / Ashley Kehr and Tony J. Robinson.
Description: Denver, CO: BiggerPockets Publishing LLC, 2023.
Identifiers: LCCN: 2023936550 | ISBN: 9781960178046 (paperback | 9781960178053 (ebook)
Subjects: LCSH Real estate investment--United States. | Investments. | Finance, Personal. | Partnership | BISAC BUSINESS & ECONOMICS / Real Estate / General | BUSINESS & ECONOMICS / Investments & Securities / Real Estate | BUSINESS & ECONOMICS / Personal Finance / Investing
Classification: LCC HD1382.5 .K44 2023 | DDC 332.63/24--dc23

Printed in Canada
MBP 10 9 8 7 6 5 4 3 2 1

Dedication

Real Estate Rookies, this book is for you. Nothing gives us more inspiration and motivation than the Real Estate Rookie community. Each and every one of you has impacted someone else's life in one way or another, whether from being a guest on the podcast, sharing your win in the Facebook group, answering a question in the BiggerPockets forums, or recommending the podcast to others. We have the privilege of being behind the mic, but it is nothing compared to the value that guests bring to the podcast and our listeners bring by taking action to change their lives.

To the three little farm boys, Maverick, Colt, and Remington,
who teach me more about life and love than
I ever could have imagined.
—Your mom, Ashley

To my wife, who gave me the confidence to bet on myself and
build the business of my dreams. And to my son,
who taught me the joy of parenthood and gave me focus
and purpose at such a young stage in life.
—Tony

TABLE OF CONTENTS

Chapter 6
PARTNERSHIP STRUCTURE 97

Chapter 7
MEMOIRS OF PARTNERSHIP 130

INTRODUCTION

— *Tony* —

A Shocking Christmas "Gift"

Several years ago, at 7:30 a.m. on December 23rd, I was sent a last-minute invite to a Zoom meeting. I didn't know it at the time, but I was about to receive the most shocking Christmas "gift" of my life. The meeting was with my direct supervisor and the HR Director of the company I was working for. You might be able to guess where this is going.

I had spent the last three and half years working for this company. I'd worked my way up the corporate ladder and had a lofty title (Senior Manager of North American Service Distribution). I oversaw a large team of 500 people that spanned eight different facilities in the U.S. and had a healthy six-figure salary to boot.

I was living what many would consider the American Dream.

But that fateful morning, I knew something was wrong. You get a last-minute invite to a meeting with HR and your boss when they have bad news to deliver. Nervous and anxious, I logged onto the call at the scheduled start time. Within the first few seconds, I knew it wouldn't end well for me. The HR Director explained that, as I'd suspected, I was being fired. It wasn't a long conversation, and I honestly didn't have much to say.

The call ended with *me* thanking *them*, awkwardly mumbling something about there being "no bad blood." After hanging up, I sat in silence for a while. A million thoughts began to race through my mind.

How could they? After everything I gave to this company, they're letting me go like this?

Then, my thoughts shifted away from anger and toward fear and anxiety.

What the hell am I going to do? How will I pay my mortgage?

I eventually got up from the chair I was sitting in and mustered up the courage to tell my wife what had just happened. She was equally shocked, and we sat in a daze for some time. Eventually, she asked, "So what do we do next?"

At the time, we had a modest real estate portfolio that consisted of four long-term rentals (two of which weren't even generating revenue because they were being rehabbed), two active short-term rentals, and one additional property under contract. We had a bit of cash flow coming in, but nothing that would replace the big six-figure salary we had just lost.

After some back and forth, weighing pros and cons, and thinking about the kind of future we wanted for ourselves, my wife and I agreed that instead of me going out and looking for another J-O-B, we should buckle down and focus on taking this real estate side-hustle and turning into a full-blown business. That same morning, I went to the desk in my home office that I'd been sitting at every day for my day job, removed my old work laptop, pulled out my personal laptop, and went to work.

While I was confident in our decision to focus 100 percent of our efforts on real estate, we now faced new challenges. First, all the money stashed away that we'd earmarked to cover down payments and closing costs for our next investments was now needed to cover our living expenses. We had enough cash saved up to last more than a year, but we couldn't really cover our living expenses *and* buy a bunch of real estate. And it's not like we could choose real estate over living!

Second, even if we did have extra cash, getting approved for favorable loans would be difficult because neither of us had W-2 income (my wife had voluntarily left her job earlier that same year).

Since we had limited resources, we had to get creative if we wanted to grow our portfolio. We shifted our entire strategy and focused on taking our skills as real estate investors and partnering with others who aspired to invest but lacked the time, ability, and desire to do it alone.

And that's exactly what we did. The morning I was fired, we had just two active short-term rentals. Twelve months later, we scaled to fifteen. And the vast majority of those properties were purchased through our creative use of partnerships.

My education in real estate partnerships wasn't something I took lightly. My livelihood—my ability to provide for my family and keep a roof over my head—forced me to become world-class at leveraging real estate partnerships to create win-win situations for everyone involved. And this book is the result of my real-world, lifesaving experience in real estate partnerships. I wrote it, of course, with a partner: my coauthor Ashley Kehr, who also complements my background in partnerships with her own. (Ashley, luckily, didn't get fired from her job, but she was also forced to figure out the world of real estate partnerships to kickstart her investing journey.)

What's on the Agenda?

Throughout this book, we (Ashley and I) will share the exact framework that we've used in our business to build real estate partnerships that create win-win situations for everyone involved.

In this book, you'll learn about real estate partnerships from all angles. We'll guide you through the process of identifying the right partner, structuring your partnerships for success, aligning objectives with your partner's, and navigating the inevitable bumps in the road that every partnership faces.

Not only will you walk away with a powerful framework for real estate partnerships but we'll also share our own experiences—both the good and the bad. Our goal is to give you a real-world, practical, and tactical guide to building your own successful real estate partnerships.

In reality, this book is also about more than partnerships. It's a guide to (and a reminder of) the transformative power of collaboration. It's about people coming together with a shared vision and commitment to supporting each other, and the impact it can have on your business and your life. Once you unlock the potential of real estate partnerships, you'll have a unique superpower that will help you to access more cash, acquire bigger deals, and achieve higher profits. Let's get started.

Chapter 1
THE MISSING PIECE

— Ashley —

Partnership, no matter the type, brings possibilities. Whether you're choosing a life partner, a business partner, an accountability partner, or a dance partner, partnership is possible in almost all aspects of life. This book focuses on business partnerships and, more specifically, real estate investing partnerships, but you'll find that many of the takeaways apply to all kinds of partnerships or relationships in life.

Before we dive into learning how to create a strong and successful partnership, how to find a partner, and how to structure the partnership, you should first consider if you actually *need* a partner. Taking on a business partner is a huge responsibility. There are many ways to get started in real estate or to continue to grow your real estate business without a partner, so let's explore some reasons you may want or need a partner.

Why Do You Want a Partner?
There are four main reasons you'll want to partner on a deal: time, money, knowledge/experience, and confidence. These four factors

are the crucial puzzle pieces to getting your next deal. Let's break each one down:

TIME

How busy are you now? Do you binge Netflix shows? Is your phone alerting you that you spent ten hours scrolling social media this past week? Is your current job taking up all of your time? Do your kids participate in every after-school activity? Do you get to take a nap each afternoon?

We each get the same twenty-four hours in a day; it all just depends on what you do with it. Everyone's circumstances and situations are different, but you need to decide if you have the time to invest in real estate on your own or if you require a partner who has the time.

Before you even start to think about whether you have the time, you need to complete a time study. There may be a few of you who are already diligent and know exactly where your time is going, but most of us don't track our hours. For those of you who think you have the time but have already checked social media twice while reading this chapter, you may want to do this little assignment.

You are going to track your time for one week (or better yet, two weeks). Start with jotting down each activity, task, or obligation you complete each day, along with the time it takes you to complete it.

A sample day might look like this:
- Twenty minutes hitting the snooze button and reading news headlines
- Thirty minutes getting ready for work
- Forty minutes driving to work (including a stop for coffee)
- Eight hours working (you could even break down your workday to see how productive it is—if you care to know)
- Forty-five minutes running errands
- Ten minutes scrolling social media in the driveway
- Twenty minutes making dinner
- Fifteen minutes eating dinner
- Fifteen minutes putting laundry away and talking on the phone
- Thirty minutes searching YouTube videos for the best movie quotes of all time

- Ninety minutes watching Netflix
- Ten minutes taking out the garbage and checking mailbox
- Fifteen minutes getting ready for bed
- Sixty minutes watching TV and scrolling social media

If you cut out the ninety minutes of Netflix and sixty minutes of TV and social media, you just gained an additional two and a half hours to research or invest in real estate. If you really want it, you'll make time for it. Sometimes just seeing a visual of how much time you spend on other activities that aren't producing income or adding value for your family can give you that extra push to change your habits.

Tracking is big in the personal finance community too. You may think you know where your money is going, but once you sit down and write out how much is going where, seeing it all on paper can be a huge eye-opener. In turn, it might make you want to cut down on expenses in order to save or pay down debt. Throughout this book, we will mention how imperative visuals can be to get a point across or to make a statement or impact on what you are trying to convey.

How you spend your time will also depend on your strategy and the type of investing you are looking to do or may be currently doing. If you have the time but don't want to spend it investing in real estate, that is perfectly fine too. Isn't that why most of us want to invest—so we can achieve that freedom of time? Isn't that the real win, not how many units you own or houses you flipped? Taking on a partner strictly to help you achieve more free time in your life is a great reason to do it. Even if you have the time, it doesn't necessarily mean you have to or want to spend it investing.

With a partnership, there will be some give and take. Obviously, you will have to give up something to entice a partner to utilize their own time; usually, that is equity, which subsequently gives up your return on the investment or profit. You just need to decide if you are the person bringing time to the puzzle or if that's where you need someone.

Remember, as the puzzle fills, you will want to add value and bring on a partner who complements what you may not be contributing to the partnership. There are no right or wrong pieces to bring to the table.

MONEY

After evaluating your time commitment, it's time to look at your money. Lift up the mattress and count those dollar bills you've been shoving under there. How much money can you comfortably put toward your next deal while still having reserves and being able to pay all your bills? Is there a sizable stash, but you are still after OPM (Other People's Money)?

If you don't have money (or you do but don't want to spend it), then finding a partner who does can be an asset to you, especially if you are bringing another piece (or pieces) to the puzzle. Maybe you're able to contribute a certain amount, but you want to invest in a more costly property. Pieces of the puzzle can be shared between partners. Keep in mind, you can also have multiple partners to complete the puzzle.

We all know that money is needed to buy real estate. However, a common misconception is that it must be *your* money. The truth is, you don't need to solely use your own money. Are there different ways you could "find" money? A couple of ways you can tap into money include the following:

- **Refinance or get a line of credit on an existing property you own that has equity in it**

  Example: A primary residence has a current mortgage of $220,000. The property appraises for $320,000. The bank states they will give you a line of credit up to 85 percent of the appraised value excluding the current mortgage balance.

  $320,000 \times 85\% = $272,000

  $272,000 - $220,000 = $52,000

  The bank would give you a line of credit for $52,000. (Of course, this also depends on your credit score and debt-to-income ratio.)

- **Get a portfolio line of credit**

  If you have a brokerage account, at certain times you can get a line of credit and use the brokerage account as collateral. There are requirements, however, including having a certain amount in your brokerage account in order to apply, maintaining a balance, and using an account that isn't a retirement account. This is often called a "portfolio line of credit." It's typical for banks to lend 30 percent of the account balance, but there are banks that will lend more than that, sometimes up to 60 percent.

Example: You have an investment brokerage account with Vanguard. This is a non-retirement account. The current balance at today's market prices is $126,459.

The bank offers you 30 percent of the current balance.

$126,459 × 30% = $37,937.70

Your line of credit is $37,937.70.

- **Borrow from your 401k**

This is money that will be pulled out of the stock market that you can use for whatever you'd like. The loan will be paid back through a deduction from your paycheck. You do have to pay interest on the loan, but since you are borrowing from your own 401k, you are technically paying yourself interest. There are, of course, limitations on how much you can borrow. As of 2022, the limit is $50,000 or 50 percent of your vested account balance.

Example: Clinch Landscaping offers a 401k retirement account where you have a balance of $64,451. When speaking with HR, you are told that you are 100 percent vested in the 401k balance. This means you have worked there long enough that the money Clinch Landscaping has contributed on your behalf as an employee benefit is 100 percent entitled to you.

You are eligible for a loan of 50 percent of the current balance.

$64,451 × 50% = $32,225.50

The loan amount you are eligible for is $32,225.50. The loan is amortized over five years and repaid with principal and interest out of your paycheck each week.

- **Find a private money lender**

Is there someone you know with money who may want to be a private money lender? Could you seek out a money lender at a meetup? A private money lender won't have equity in the deal and won't be your business partner. This is a business relationship, but they aren't tied to you like a business partner would be. You would pay them a set return on their money or even offer them a profit share (which can be structured in many ways depending on what you negotiate), but they wouldn't be an owner of the company or property.

Example: Remington has a friend who has just retired and sold his company. Remington approaches his friend and asks him if he knows anyone who is looking to invest their money in real estate instead of having it sit in a bank. Remington's friend says, "Well, actually, *I* am looking to do that." Remington borrows $100,000 from his friend to purchase a duplex and will pay his friend (now acting as a private money lender) 6 percent interest over ten years. Remington's attorney files a mortgage stating that the friend is the mortgage holder and has a lien on the property until repayment is made in full. Remington is the full owner of the property and makes monthly mortgage payments to his friend.

Those are just a few ways you can find the money for your deal. If you're not interested in having a business partner and are simply doing it because you think you need money to fund your deal, make sure you explore all other possible options first. By forcing yourself to enter into a partnership when your heart isn't in it, you're building that partnership on a shaky foundation and setting it up for failure.

KNOWLEDGE/EXPERIENCE

Knowledge and experience are similar concepts, but it's worthwhile to explain the differences between the two.

Knowledge comes from *learning*. You gain knowledge from spending hours interacting on the BiggerPockets forums, reading BiggerPockets books, and listening to the *Real Estate Rookie* podcast.

Experience comes from *doing*. You gain experience by analyzing deals, project-managing your rehabs, catering to the guests at your short-term rental, and working with tenants at your long-term rental.

But here's the truth about the world of real estate investing: It's massive, and there are so many disciplines. There are some investors who have massive amounts of experience in one discipline (like house flipping), but they might be completely clueless in another discipline (like small, multifamily).

This means that in a partnership, experience is obviously incredibly helpful, but simply having the right knowledge can have a big impact as well.

For example, let's say you want to transition from house flipping to short-term rentals. Even though you're exceptionally good at finding off-market deals, managing rehabs, and sticking to budgets, you know nothing about designing a property, managing guests, or using pricing tools.

Aside from quickly gaining all of that short-term rental knowledge yourself, you have two options: You can either partner with someone else who has the knowledge and experience to manage short-term rentals, or you can outsource it to someone who works for you as an employee or contractor who already has the knowledge.

There are pros and cons to each option. When you create a real estate partnership, often you're giving up equity in the deal. Then when you outsource it, you must be able to absorb the cost of that person.

As you build and scale your real estate business, there will always be gaps in your knowledge and experience. Deciding between partnering and outsourcing comes down to which strategy aligns most with what you want. Again, since the world of real estate investing is so expansive, it's unrealistic to think that any one person can master *all* disciplines; this is why partnerships are so useful and powerful. They allow you to shortcut the amount of time it takes to acquire knowledge and build your experience.

If you're reading this and feel you already have enough knowledge and experience to get started, but for some reason haven't been able to pull the trigger on a deal, then it's possible something else is holding you back—perhaps the fear that you don't actually know what to do. That leads us to our fourth puzzle piece: confidence.

CONFIDENCE

As hosts of the *Real Estate Rookie* podcast, we've been fortunate to talk with hundreds of aspiring real estate investors. One of the most common statements we hear from guests is that they've read all the books, listened to all of the podcasts, and watched all of the YouTube videos, yet they just can't shake the fear that there's still something they don't know or that there's still more they need to learn. They might feel uneasy that their investment won't be successful or afraid that something will go wrong.

If this sounds like you, let's explore some ways you can get rid of that fear for good.

One way is by bringing on a partner who has solutions to the problems you might encounter. Even the most experienced investors struggle with fear, especially when venturing into bigger deals. Partnerships offer a way to minimize risk. This ties into the previous puzzle piece: If you partner with someone who has the right experience, the partnership then increases your confidence and reduces the perceived risk.

Have you ever been in a situation where partnering up with someone made things just a *little* less scary and gave you the confidence to move forward? Maybe it's going to a meetup and walking in with a friend instead of walking in by yourself and not knowing anyone. Or maybe it's jumping off a two-story rock with someone rather than alone. Simply having someone by your side can increase your confidence.

There are a couple of different aspects of this confidence piece, which we'll explain later in the chapter, but let's go over an example first.

My first partner played a critical role in this puzzle piece. I was terrified of something terrible happening. What was that terrible thing? I truly didn't know, but it was something along the lines of a tenant falling down the stairs and suing me, or the wind blowing the roof off the top of my house. These are all reasonable scenarios to lie awake at night and ponder, right?

To help ease those fears (and sleep better at night), I took on my first partner. Throughout this book, we'll refer to my first partner as Evan, because that's his real name and he deserves a little recognition. Evan had resources that I didn't (like money). By partnering with him, I was able to mitigate that particular risk.

The first way Evan boosted my confidence and helped me get over my fear was by trusting me to invest his life's savings into my first real estate investment. That was a major boost to my confidence because, at that point, it wasn't just me who had vetted the deal and believed in it. Evan also vetted it and believed in it enough to put in all the money he had to buy the deal. That made me think, *Okay, I must be on to something.*

Secondly, between the two of us we had enough brainpower, adequate resources, and a network of people (mostly Evan's at this time) to solve any of those worst-case scenarios that were keeping me up at night. His network and net worth made this deal possible.

Assembling the Four Pieces of the Puzzle

To ensure that you both *want* and *need* a partner and to start creating a strong foundation for a partnership, go over the four pieces of the puzzle—time, money, knowledge/experience, and confidence—and decide which ones you think you are missing or need fulfilling. Fill in the table below and for each puzzle piece state whether you already possess that piece. Be sure to explain the *why* behind each answer.

PUZZLE PIECE	EXAMPLE	YOUR RESPONSE
Time	I work a nine to five job and focus on real estate from 7:00 p.m. to 9:00 p.m. on most weekdays and from 4:00 p.m. to 8:00 p.m. on Sunday evenings.	
Money	All of my money is invested into a property I am currently flipping. I don't have the funds to purchase another deal.	

Knowledge/ Experience	I have flipped three houses and have the experience and knowledge to complete another one. I have a reliable contractor on my team and have a deal picked out. I don't know how to create the best system and processes to make flipping more efficient to grow and scale.
Confidence	I am confident I can flip another house. My only fear is that I am taking on too much risk by flipping multiple homes at once without enough in reserves.

Taking on a partner is more than just figuring out who needs what from the other; it's a relationship. You have to work together, and that's not always easy. Even if it's going to be completely passive for one investor, there will still be decisions that need to be made together and responsibilities you'll share with one another. Are you willing to make that commitment?

Even if you are just bringing the money and need someone else to provide the other pieces, you still have a responsibility. It's easy to think, *Well, they are obligated to me because they had better do whatever it takes to not lose my money*, but you have the responsibility of getting the money to them, and, depending on how the deal is structured, that could mean possibly putting more money into the deal and avoiding trouble that could impact your business for the partnership.

There's a joke that goes around that it's often more difficult to separate from a business partnership than a marriage. At least marriage laws are in place within your state, so you have an idea of what will happen! Meanwhile, if you don't have proper documentation for your partnership, everything could be up in the air if a split between you and your partner happens. We'll discuss documentation in Chapter 6.

The Final Perk

There is another aspect to deciding if you want a partner that really isn't a puzzle piece, since it's not necessary to get your deal done. It's more of a perk.

It's about not being in it alone.

There are people (including me) who thrive from working with others. I love brainstorming ideas, the thrill of celebrating wins, working out solutions together, sharing the risk, and being able to rely on each other. There is great benefit in surrounding yourself with like-minded individuals, especially if you each own the same type of business; you have the same goals and mutually benefit from doing the best you can. A person could attend a mastermind event or have an accountability partner, but no one will be as dedicated to the success of that business as someone who has equity in it. Mastermind events and accountability partners are awesome and have their own impact on your business, but they're different from what a partner can bring to the table.

To highlight the differences, let's break down what an accountability partner is and how it compares to having a business partner. An accountability partner—a good one, at least—calls you out on all your crap and is your biggest hype person (that's the informal definition). This person will keep you on track, check in with you, and make you want to do what you say you'll do so you don't disappoint them. The most important part about having an accountability partner is that you reciprocate all of those things: You check in with them, you hype them up, you call them out when they aren't doing what they promised to do to improve their business or themselves. This person really doesn't need to know the ins and outs of your business and has no benefit from your business thriving or dying.

A business partner, on the other hand, does. They are also at risk if you don't perform or do the things you say you'll do. Your actions affect the outcome of the deal, which in turn affects all of the owners of the deal.

The Partnership Pyramid

One of the most common questions asked by those seeking a partner is how to structure the partnership. It's a great question, and I promise we will answer it in detail in Chapter 6. There are many other factors to consider besides the structure, however, all of which we will cover throughout the book.

To help you better understand all of the elements you should consider when partnering, we've created a framework called the Partnership Pyramid. The Partnership Pyramid is a visual representation of the layers that make up a successful real estate partnership. Each layer builds upon the layer below it, and as you master each layer you increase the chances of making your partnership successful.

The three layers of the Partnership Pyramid are Goals, Structure, and Communication. There are tactical pieces and key action items that need to take place for each layer.

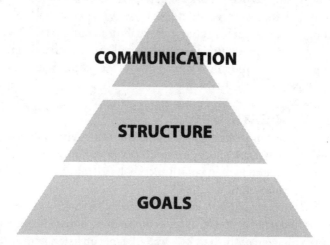

GOALS

The first layer of the Partnership Pyramid is Goals. When we talk about goals in a real estate partnership, we're trying to understand how aligned the two partners are: Are they on the same page and moving toward the same goals? Do they share the same long-term vision for the partnership?

In Chapter 5, we'll explain how you and your partner can establish shared goals and create alignment. But before you can work on goal setting within your partnership, you have to truly understand yourself and identify your unique skills and abilities. Ultimately, you should understand the value that you bring to a partnership and the ways you can help that partnership achieve its goals. In Chapter 2, we'll walk you through the exact steps you need to truly understand all of the ways you can provide value to a partnership.

STRUCTURE

Structure is the next layer of the Partnership Pyramid. It refers to the agreement between the two partners as to each partner's specific roles and responsibilities within the partnership, along with the ownership terms. All of Chapter 6 is dedicated to showing you how to structure your real estate partnership. There is no "right" or "wrong" way to structure your partnership, so our goal in Chapter 6 is to give you a solid understanding of all the elements that make up a partnership and allow you to choose the pieces that make the most sense for your situation.

COMMUNICATION

Communication is the final component of the pyramid. No relationship can thrive without clear and concise communication. How many circumstances can you think of where things didn't go well because of miscommunication?

It's important to note that communication isn't always just talking and sharing what's on your mind. Often, solid communication in a partnership comes down to how well each of you listen to the other. Listening without being worried or focused on what you are going to say next is an important skill to develop. Have you caught yourself planning what you'll say next before the other person even finishes their sentence? How can you actually pay attention to what someone else is saying if your mind is distracted by what you plan to say next?

Chapter 9 is all about establishing effective communication within your partnership.

BUILDING THE PYRAMID

As you create your partnership, keep these three layers of the Partnership Pyramid in mind. This book will help you successfully build each layer so that all the fundamentals are in place for a solid working relationship with your partner. There are many aspects of a partnership that will make it succeed, but, like anything else, you need a strong foundation to hold it all together.

Are You Ready for a Partner?

Let's close out this chapter with one more anecdote.

I hired a home inspector for my first investment property: a duplex. The home inspector, Lloyd, asked me about myself and the property. He was thrilled to hear it was going to be my first investment and told me he'd built a portfolio of investment properties several years ago with a partner; unfortunately, he had had to sell them all. Lloyd went on to explain that his partner was getting a divorce. In New York state, marital assets are divided 50/50. The partner could not afford to pay his wife 50 percent and keep his equity in the properties, so they sold the properties and he split the sale proceeds with his wife for his percentage.

Lloyd hadn't reinvested his proceeds from the sale and told me how much he wished he still owned the properties. At the time, I didn't know to ask more questions: Did you have an operating agreement that stated what would happen in the event one of the partners wanted to sell and the other didn't? Would you have been able to refinance some of the properties instead of selling them? Questions now swirl in my head so I can protect myself should that exact scenario happen to me.

The easy answer would be for neither partner to ever get married. However, I have learned a lot over the years, and I know there are better ways to protect yourself than demanding your partner never marry! This is just one scenario in which a partnership can go wrong, and you have no control over the situation (like someone else's divorce affecting you).

Are you ready for those curveballs? Do you still want a partner? Hopefully you will keep reading and implementing the information in this book, so you'll already have solutions to these worst-case scenario issues before they arise.

Now that you have decided you want a partner, how can *you* add value to that partnership? We'll spend the next chapter discussing this very question, which is critical to your goal-setting foundation. It's something you want to ponder and evaluate before you even start to inquire about what exactly a partner will do for you.

REAL-LIFE PARTNERSHIPS
Joseph Breamer
INVESTS IN: Tennessee

Network, time, and money: these are the three ingredients necessary for a deal and profitable partnership. This three-way partnership consists of:

- PARTNER 1: Has access to off-market deals and local network expertise in the markets he operates in.
- ME AND MY WIFE: Run a successful short-term rental cohosting company and have the time and passion to self-manage short-term rentals.
- PARTNER 2: Brings capital and the urge to grow his portfolio.

The off-market short-term rentals come from Partner 1, the capital comes from Partner 2, and the management comes from my wife and me. Put all the ingredients together, and we make a beautiful dish powered by partnerships!

Chapter 2
WILL I ADD VALUE AS A PARTNER?

— *Tony* —

Whether it's from a seasoned investor who's looking to partner for the first time or a rookie investor seeking their first deal, a common question is always "Why would anyone want to partner with me?"

Throughout this chapter, we'll explore all the ways you can provide value to a partnership so you can confidently approach potential partners, knowing it'll be a win-win for everyone involved.

Three Pillars of Partnership Value

There are three key ways you can provide value to a partnership. We'll call these the Three Pillars of Partnership Value. The first pillar is your personality (who you are). The second pillar is your resources (what you have), and the third pillar is your operational focus (what you'll do).

By discussing these three pillars with your potential partner, you'll better understand the value each of you brings to the table.

It's essential that you both clearly understand the importance the other person provides to prevent issues down the road.

Nothing can derail a partnership faster than one partner feeling that they bring more value to the table than their partner and that the partnership structure doesn't correctly compensate them and reflect their value. But when you both discuss and can agree on the value that each person brings, it makes it much easier to structure the partnership fairly and equitably.

In my own business, my partner and I failed to have this discussion and understanding around value at the outset; we just jumped in and started working. My primary business partnership includes me, my wife, and our third partner. When we started the business, my wife wasn't super involved in it, so the initial agreement was that I owned 50 percent of the company and the third partner owned 50 percent. That seemed fair at the time because I was essentially doing 50 percent of the work, and he was doing 50 percent of the work.

But as we grew and scaled, my wife became a critical part of the business. Over time, we were each doing about a third of the work. And honestly, there were moments when my wife was doing more work than me and our other partner combined.

As the business matured, my wife became the owner of the operations. She managed guest communications (our business is in the short-term rental space), managed our rehab and maintenance crews, designed our properties, and was the lead person setting up all of the properties. That's a *ton* of work. And when she first joined the team, we all assumed she'd just be answering a few messages on the Airbnb app. But that's how partnerships go: When you start a new partnership, you make assumptions about workload. Sometimes those assumptions are spot-on, and other times they are way, way off.

But even though our third partner was doing a third of the work, he was still receiving 50 percent of the profits. We all had to sit down and have a candid and somewhat uncomfortable conversation addressing the fact that the value my wife and I were bringing to the table was no longer accurately reflected in our partnership structure.

We had to walk through all of the responsibilities that my wife had taken on. We ultimately agreed on a structure that made sense for everyone.

You can avoid tough conversations by clarifying the value each of you will bring to the partnership.

Now we'll dive deeper into each of the Three Pillars of Partnership Value.

ADDING VALUE WITH YOUR PERSONALITY

When people think of real estate partnerships, they often think of who's doing what tasks and who's bringing the money. And while those are essential parts of any real estate partnership (and we'll talk about both of those in a bit), I want to start this conversation about adding value in a slightly unusual place: your personality!

Personality is the first Pillar of Partnership Value, and we start here because the right blend of personalities can make a real estate partnership unstoppable. In his book *Traction*, author Gino Wickman describes how two personality types have combined to create almost every majorly successful company we can think of: Apple, Microsoft, Facebook, and many more.

Wickman states that you need two types of personalities heading any business if you want it to be successful: First, you need a Visionary. The Visionary is the person who conceived the idea of the business and the one who typically comes up with the big-picture ideas for the future of the business. Secondly, you need an Integrator. The Integrator is the "glue person" who focuses on the day-to-day execution of the business. They take the big-picture ideas from the Visionary and boil them down into "action plans" for the company to execute. The dynamic duo of the Visionary and the Integrator drives the company toward success.

Take us, the authors of this book, for example. I (Tony) am a textbook Visionary. I'm great at dreaming up big, ambitious goals. Almost to a fault, I envision the next big idea. But I struggle with the details. Ashley, on the other hand, is an Integrator who has the tendencies of a Visionary. Her strong suit is integrating, but when necessary, she can tap into the vision. She has a hard time creating long-term visions, but she's great at creating short-term visions and then executing them.

Real estate partnerships need these personality types to succeed. But again, you want the right blend of personalities to ensure that the partnership is well-rounded and that the weaknesses of one partner are covered by the strengths of the other, and vice versa.

Now that you understand why personalities are so important in creating a successful real estate partnership, let's talk through how you can identify your own personality, behaviors, and tendencies and use that information to find the perfect partner.

Using Personality Tests

I love a good personality test. Most people are subconsciously aware of their personality traits and character tendencies, but a good personality test brings that awareness to a conscious level. It can help put words and a framework to who you are as a person, how you operate, and what's important to you.

In my personal life, my wife and I took a personality test to understand our romantic relationship tendencies. The test came from a fantastic book called *The Five Love Languages* by Gary Chapman. Chapman said that most people in relationships prefer to give and receive expressions of love from their partner in five different ways: Gifts, Quality Time, Physical Touch, Acts of Service, and Words of Affirmation.

After reading that book, a light bulb went on for my wife and me. We both knew subconsciously how we wanted to receive love, but we never had the words to express those wants clearly. Thanks to the book, it became clear to us what each of our hearts really wanted from the other person.

My wife's primary love language is Quality Time, which means for her to feel loved by me she needs me physically near her, with my attention focused on her and what we're doing at that moment. My love languages are evenly split between Acts of Service and Words of Affirmation. For me, as long as you do nice things for me and say nice things to me, I feel loved.

Now, notice our love languages aren't the same. And most people tend to *give* love in the same way they want to *receive* love. Can you see where the disconnect lies here?

I was trying to show my wife love by cleaning the house, washing the cars, and telling her how beautiful she was, but she wanted to show me love by sitting with me in the office when I was supposed to be working. Once we read the book, we both clearly understood how the other person wanted to be loved. Now I know when I need to put my laptop down, lock the door to the office, and spend the evening doing nothing but being in her presence. And now she knows how much I appreciate it when she does little things like cook breakfast or tell me how much she enjoyed that last podcast episode I recorded. We love each other more deeply by better understanding each other's tendencies and personality traits.

Now, you might be thinking, *What the heck does loving your wife have to do with me and my real estate partnerships?* The answer is, More than you probably think. You see, although your real estate partnership won't be a romantic relationship, it is still very much a relationship.

A relationship is defined as "a state of affairs existing between those having relations or dealings." With that definition, hopefully, it becomes 100 percent clear that you *will* be in a relationship when you enter into a partnership. While understanding that partner's love language may not be necessary, understanding that person's traits and tendencies is exceptionally important. Even if your partner isn't your lover, it can still be beneficial to show appreciation and gratitude through gift giving or quality time. This could be purchasing a new golf club for your partner when he solves an issue that will save the company money or taking him to dinner to spend quality time.

Luckily for you, there are tons of personality tests that will allow you and your partner to unlock a deeper understanding of one another and ultimately create a stronger foundation for your partnership.

The DISC Assessment

The personality test I've come to enjoy the most is called the DISC assessment. Although it gained popularity in the last decade, the DISC originated in the late 1920s. Psychologist William Moulton

Marston (who also created an early version of the lie detector test and was inducted into the comic book hall of fame for creating Wonder Woman) detailed the theory of four distinct personality types in his book *Emotions of Normal People*.

Each of the four letters in DISC stands for a unique behavioral style: Decisive, Interactive, Stabilizing, and Cautious. (Note: Depending on which DISC assessment you take, you may see different words defining these four letters, but the underlying behavioral styles are roughly the same.)

The assessment I'll reference throughout this section comes from the Innermetrix DISC Plus Profile by Jay Niblick. I prefer this to many of the other DISC assessments because it combines the DISC index with a values index, giving you a clear understanding of both *how* you like to get things done and *why* you're motivated to get those things done.

Today, the DISC assessment is widely used in the business world to help employers select candidates for open roles and to better understand their current employees' strengths and weaknesses. But it's also incredibly useful for anyone interested in a real estate partnership.

Let's break down what each of these four behavioral styles means. And to clarify, these four behavioral styles each represent a range, not a yes or no. For example, you could be high on the Decisive scale, low on the Decisive scale, or somewhere in the middle.

■ Decisive

This personality trait details one's preference for solving problems and getting results.

Niblick defines someone who's a High D as the following:

Tend to solve new problems very quickly and assertively. They take an active and direct approach to obtaining results. The key here is new problems such as those that are unprecedented or haven't happened before. There may also be an element of risk in taking the wrong approach or developing an incorrect solution, but those with a High D score are willing to take those risks, even if they may be incorrect.

And Niblick defines someone who's a Low D as the following:

Tend to solve new problems in a more deliberate, controlled, and organized manner. Again, the key here is new and unprecedented problems. The Lower D style will solve routine problems very quickly because the outcomes are already known. But when the outcomes are unknown and the problem is an uncertain one, the Lower D style will approach the new problem in a calculated and deliberate manner by thinking things through very carefully before acting.

What a High D Can Bring to a Real Estate Partnership

A High D is going to thrive in any situation where their forceful nature, assertiveness, and quick action taking will be valued. In a real estate partnership, your High D could be the person negotiating your deals, because you know they're not going to back down from the person on the other side of the table. A High D could also work well as a manager for any rehab projects. Their ability to give clear and direct communication combined with their desire to make quick decisions and move fast may allow them to do well in managing subcontractors and handymen.

■ Interactive

This personality trait details one's preference for interacting with others and showing emotions.

Niblick defines someone who's a High I as the following:

Tend to meet new people in an outgoing, gregarious, and socially assertive manner. The key here is new people whom one hasn't met before. Many other styles are talkative, but more so with people that they've known for some time. The Higher I scorers are talkative, interactive, and open, even with people whom they have just initially met. People scoring in this range may also be a bit impulsive. Generally speaking, those with the Higher I scores are talkative and outgoing.

And Niblick defines someone who's a Low I as the following:

Tend to meet new people in a more controlled, quiet, and reserved manner. Here's where the key term "new people" enters the equation. Those with Lower I scores are talkative with their friends and close associates, but tend to be more reserved with people they've just recently met. They tend to place a premium on the control of emotions, and approach new relationships with a more reflective approach than an emotional one.

What a High I Can Bring to a Real Estate Partnership

High I's and High D's tend to be more extroverted. While the High D can sometimes be seen as abrasive, the High I is a bit more enthusiastic and persuasive. They also thrive in making new relationships, which is key in the real estate business.

That kind of skill set would make a High I a great candidate for anything people-related. A High I could be the property manager for a property with tenants who need a high level of care. Or it could be the person who handles all of the direct-to-seller marketing. This person could be the cold-caller, door-knocker, and closer. Their persuasiveness and genuine enjoyment in connecting with new people might allow them to close more deals than someone who's a Low I.

A High I could also make for a great fundraiser. They have the desire to go out to networking events like meetups and conferences, put themselves out there, and make new connections.

■ Stabilizing

This personality trait details one's preference for pacing, persistence, and steadiness.

Niblick defines someone who's a High S as the following:

Tend to prefer a more controlled, deliberative, and predictable environment. They place a premium on security of a work situation and disciplined behavior. They also tend to show a sense of loyalty to a team or organization, and as a result, may have a greater longevity or tenure in a position than some other styles. They have an excellent listening style and are very patient coaches and teachers for others on the team.

And Niblick defines someone who's a Low S as the following:

Tend to prefer a more flexible, dynamic, unstructured work environment. They value freedom of expression and the ability to change quickly from one activity to another. They tend to become bored with the same routine that brings security to the Higher S. As a result, they will seek opportunities and outlets for their high sense of urgency and high activity levels, as they have a preference for spontaneity.

What a High S Can Bring to a Real Estate Partnership

The High S would operate well in a position where there's clear direction, clear expectations, and a predictable environment. In your real estate partnership, this could mean a number of things. The High S could be the person who manages the books or handles invoicing, or perhaps they analyze the deals or markets. This person will basically thrive in any role where they can move at their own pace.

■ Cautious

This personality trait details one's preference for procedures, standards, and protocols.

Niblick defines someone who's a High C as the following:

Tend to adhere to rules, standards, procedures, and protocol set by those in authority whom they respect. They like things to be done the right way according to the operating manual. "Rules are made to be followed" is an appropriate motto for those with High C scores. They have some of the highest quality control interests of any of the styles and frequently wish others would do the same.

And Niblick defines someone who's a Low C as the following:

Tend to operate more independently from the rules and standard operating procedures. They tend to be bottom-line oriented. If they find an easier way to do something, they'll do it by developing a variety of strategies as situations demand. To the Lower C scorers, rules are only guidelines, and may be bent or broken as necessary to obtain results.

What a High C Can Bring to a Real Estate Partnership

In any real estate partnership, it's always helpful to have one "dreamer" and one "doer." A High C is similar to a High S, but where the High S likes to operate *within* systems and processes, the High C wants to *create* those systems and processes.

Because the High C values procedures and standards, this person would perform well in any role that needs systems and processes. They can form an effective duo with a High I when it comes to property management. The High I can handle all of the people-related tasks (talking with tenants and contractors), and the High C can create all the systems and processes for the back of the house (how those tenants pay rent and how those contractors should submit their bids).

Some examples of High C tasks might be creating the template for your Scope of Work for your rehabs, creating the processes for turning a unit once a tenant moves out, and setting up the software tools that are needed for your business and then training others on how to use them.

Identify Your and Your Partner's Strengths and Weaknesses

Whether you use the DISC, take other personality tests, or just do some deep reflection, take the time to try to identify your strengths and weaknesses, both from a behavioral standpoint and a tactical standpoint.

If you haven't yet identified a potential partner—or even if you have—be sure to dig deep with them about their own strengths and weaknesses.

It would be terrible if you became partners with someone who had the same exact weaknesses as you do. Imagine if both of you were Low C's who hate structure and processes. There would be systems in place to run the business, but every time a routine problem popped up, it would become an emergency because no one ever thought to write down how the problem was handled the last ten times it happened. Or perhaps both of you would brainstorm amazing ideas around how to grow the portfolio, but since neither partner took the time to actually strategize *how* to make those ideas a reality, the portfolio would grow at a much slower pace.

Now imagine if both you and your partner were High D's. Alone, a High D might be a fantastic leader and CEO, but two High D's together? There's a high likelihood that both people would be jockeying for control. They'd both want the final say, and they'd both be quick to make decisions and take big risks.

When both you and your partner are acutely aware of what your strengths and weaknesses are, it allows you to work better together. Spending time focusing on who you are and how you operate is some of the best personal development work you can do. The better you understand yourself, the better you become at working effectively with others. If you know how you communicate best with others, you can let your partner know.

Besides the DISC personality test, another beneficial measure of your personality is the Enneagram. According to this assessment, there are nine different personality types that most people fall into. Not only will this help you better understand yourself, but you'll also gain insight into the people around you.

Listen to Enneagram expert Nick Baumgart on the *Real Estate Rookie* podcast!

Not everyone likes to interact, communicate, or be treated the same way. Both the Enneagram and the DISC assessment are tools that can help you and your partner better understand how to interact and communicate with each and treat each other.

ADDING VALUE WITH YOUR RESOURCES

Now that you understand how you can add value to a partnership with your personality, it's time to move to the second Pillar of Partnership Value: your resources.

Purchasing and successfully managing any real estate deal requires five resources: capital, bankability, ability, time, and desire. You can either bring all five resources to the table yourself or find a partner who can bring the resources you're lacking.

Understanding these five resources will help you better identify what you should be looking for in a potential partner, so let's go through each one.

Capital

Capital is the first resource, and it's one of the most critical. When we say "capital," we're talking about how much money a person has *readily available* to invest into a real estate deal.

Capital is so important because you can't close on a real estate transaction without money. That said, notice I said capital is *one* of the most critical resources. Capital is not the only resource that's important. This is because someone can have enough money to buy a real estate deal but still be short on some of the other critical resources that are needed, which we'll touch on next.

It's easy for the person who contributed all, or the majority, of the capital to feel like they're in the driver's seat, and the person who didn't bring the capital may feel like the other person did them a favor. That's a dangerous dynamic in a partnership because it can be a breeding ground for resentment down the road.

Imagine how it would feel if you found a deal, managed the rehab, and managed the tenants, but you didn't have enough money to buy the deal, so you brought in a capital partner who gets 95 percent of the profits while you get 5 percent. Could you imagine being unhappy down the road? Of course you could!

So, while we all can agree that capital is important, it's not the *only* thing that's important.

Bankability

Bankability, or being "bankable," is the second resource, and it refers to the ability to get approved for a mortgage. To be bankable, that person typically will have a strong credit score, low debt-to-income ratio, and verifiable income.

Being bankable and having capital don't always go hand in hand; just because someone has capital doesn't necessarily mean that they're bankable. I've seen it happen many times; maybe they inherited a large sum of money, but their credit is shot. Or maybe they recently left their job. Perhaps they're self-employed and write off everything, which means they have little to no income on paper. There are many reasons why someone may have capital but not be in a position to get approved for a mortgage.

If someone has a strong balance sheet that allows them to get approved for a loan, or multiple loans, that can be an extremely valuable resource for a partnership.

This is what led me to my first partnership; I had one long-term rental under my belt, but I also had a mortgage for my primary residence. When I went to get my second rental property, the bank told me my debt-to-income ratio wouldn't allow for a second rental property. I had the capital, the deal, the contractor, and the property manager; I just needed the loan. I went out and found a partner who was willing to go on the mortgage application with me. Problem solved.

If you're worried that you don't know anyone who can get approved for a loan or how to find them, we'll be covering finding potential partners in Chapter 3. And if you're wondering how that partnership should be structured, we'll spend all of Chapter 6 discussing that.

Ability

Ability is the third resource, and it's defined as the possession of the means or skill to do something. In a real estate partnership, your ability is a measure of the amount of knowledge, skill, and capacity to learn that you bring to the table.

Knowledge measures how smart you are, while skill measures your ability to do those things that you're knowledgeable about. For example, a med student might be knowledgeable in triple bypass surgery, but he won't be skilled until he's completed his residency and done many actual surgeries himself.

Capacity to learn is a trait that's often overlooked. Capacity doesn't measure how smart or skillful you are *today*, but rather asks how smart or skillful you will be *tomorrow*. Capacity is measuring how able you are to add to your current knowledge and skill.

In a real estate partnership, you need at least one of these three. If, between the two of you, the partnership has no knowledge of how to invest in real estate, no skills that are relevant to investing in real estate, and no capacity to learn, then the partnership is dead in the water.

Time

Imagine that someone has $1 million in the bank, an 800 credit score, and the ability to close and manage a real estate deal on their own. At first glance, it might seem like this person has absolutely no need to partner with someone else.

But there's a missing ingredient we haven't talked about, and that's the fourth resource: time. When we say "time," we're talking about how much time that person actually has available to allocate to this specific real estate deal. What if this person has a high-paying job that demands 80-hour workweeks, or time-consuming commitments to their family, hobbies, and community? What if this person travels 340 days out of the year? It means that no matter how skilled they are or how much money they have, they probably just don't have enough time to dedicate to growing their real estate business.

This means, more likely than not, that you're going to need to find a partner who does have the time. And while capital is the resource that's oftentimes overvalued, time is the resource that's oftentimes undervalued. If one of the partners puts up the money and nothing else, and then the other partner dedicates 20 hours a week to managing the real estate business, in the long run, which partner provides more value?

Sure, the money partner allowed the deal to happen, but the partner who invested the *time* is the one who made the deal profitable and allowed the capital partner to get a return on that initial investment.

Desire

The last way that you can add value to a partnership is with desire. Even if someone has all the money and time in the world, and is exceptionally skilled at investing in real estate, if they don't have the desire to do it, then none of those other things matter.

Understanding this one distinction has been a critical part of my growth with Alpha Geek Capital. We've built a substantial short-term rental portfolio by partnering with investors who have had the time and the capital but not the *desire* to run an Airbnb business. Many of these partners could go out and find their own properties, come up with the design, put all the furniture together, manage the cleaners, manage the repairs and maintenance, communicate with the guests, and manage the pricing—but the truth is, they just don't want to.

And because the desire is absent, they're more than happy to bring their capital into our partnership, allowing them to still invest in Airbnbs but without all of the headache that usually comes along with it.

So, if you're looking for a partner, this is one key piece to focus on. Who has the actual desire to do the work that you hate doing?

Here's an example from my partnership. I love analyzing deals, but I hate setting up utilities and paying vendors. I found a partner who doesn't enjoy analyzing deals but doesn't mind being on hold with the electric company for thirty minutes to turn on the electricity at the property. We're a match made in heaven.

An action item that you can complete right now—besides taking a personality test—is to start a list of what you are good at. What are your strengths? Don't limit yourself to real estate or business strengths in general, such as being good at negotiating or analyzing deals. Take strengths from your everyday life, even miniscule things. Are you efficient at multitasking or have a high level of patience?

Once you've made this list, cross-reference it with things that you desire to do. Just because you're a strong writer and communicate well through email doesn't mean you necessarily *enjoy* writing.

So be honest with yourself. Do you detest having to respond to emails? Maybe you shouldn't be the main point of contact in the partnership. This can also go the other way. Perhaps you love shopping to furnish a short-term rental, but you're not very good at it—as in maybe it would take you ten times longer than someone else and you might not have the right eye for design that will be marketable for your rental.

Find that balance between skill and desire when deciding what roles you and your partner will play and what tasks you will take on. Note: You can hire virtual assistants from Upwork or Fivver to take over some of the miniscule tasks that maybe no partner wants to do.

ADDING VALUE WITH YOUR OPERATIONAL FOCUS

So far, we've discussed how you can add value with your personality and with your resources. Now we'll talk about how you can add value with your operational focus.

Investing in real estate is a process that entails literally hundreds of steps. Some are big, some small, some quick, and some slow. And all of those steps can be broadly placed into one of two categories: acquisitions (activities before the close) or operations (activities after the close).

It's important for you to understand which parts of that process you're uniquely qualified to do. Think back to the previous section on resources and ask yourself, What steps and action items can I apply my resources toward with the highest impact and least effort?

Let's dive into the two categories and detail some of the responsibilities that typically fall into each one.

Acquisitions

Acquisitions includes all the activities that happen before you take ownership of the property. This includes tasks like analyzing markets, finding deals, and analyzing deals. Each of these responsibilities requires a slightly different skill set.

■ Analyzing Deals & Markets

You can't (or rather, shouldn't) buy an investment without doing some degree of analysis. You want to make sure that the market is a good one to invest in and that the property itself is profitable. If you love crunching numbers and building spread-sheets, then this might be a great way for you to provide value to the partnership. (Scan the QR Code to get Ashley's book *Real Estate Rookie: 90 Days to Your First Investment*, which will teach you the basics of analyzing deals and markets.)

Typical Duties
- Reviewing large amounts of data
- Using comps to determine property values
- Building models for analysis

■ Finding Deals

There are many different ways that real estate investors find deals to invest in; some are easy (using the MLS) and others are a bit more complicated (building direct-to-seller marketing machines). Either way, someone has to be in charge of finding the deals that eventually get purchased. And usually, finding good deals revolves around building relationships with the right people. If you're the type of person who's energized by meeting with and talking to tons of new people, then this might be your way of providing value to the partnership.

Typical Duties
- Cold-calling property owners
- Going on sales appointments with property owners
- Networking with realtors and wholesalers

Operations

Operations includes everything that happens after the property is purchased. Oftentimes, this is when the hard work begins. Just because someone can get approved for a loan and find a property doesn't mean that person has the skill to take that property and make it profitable. Operations is the part of the process that makes the property profitable. It includes jobs like managing rehabs, property management, vendor management, and bookkeeping. It's all the tasks and duties that "keep the lights on."

■ Finances

Which partner is more detail-oriented and numbers-driven? Someone will need to manage the books, track income and expenses, and keep tabs on the overall financial health of the business.

Typical Duties
- Bookkeeping
- Budgeting
- Managing payables

■ Vendor and Project Management

Managing people is a necessary part of being a real estate investor. Who will be responsible for managing your plumbers, landscapers, electricians, contractors, and handymen? This could also include being responsible for managing rehab projects.

Typical Duties
- Inspecting rehab jobs
- Finding skilled laborers
- Negotiating labor costs
- Managing timelines

■ Tenant Management

If you're planning to self-manage your property, someone is going to have to be the point of contact for the tenants. This job isn't for the faint of heart.

Typical Duties
- Dealing with tenant complaints
- Leasing units
- Understanding local landlord laws
- Managing evictions

Battling Imposter Syndrome

I'd like to share a personal story with you.

I remember when I was first offered the position as the cohost for the BiggerPockets *Real Estate Rookie* podcast. At the time, I had four long-term rentals and two short-term rentals. I was equally excited and terrified about cohosting. I was excited because I understood the amazing opportunity that was being offered to me, but I was terrified because I just didn't feel worthy of the position.

I was afraid that I would record that first podcast episode and the listeners would rebel because I wasn't a "real investor." And it wasn't because the team at BiggerPockets or Ashley, my cohost, made me feel that way. It was the voice inside my head telling me, *You're not good enough*.

I had to remind myself that even though I didn't have 1,000 units, I had six. To the person who has zero units, I can probably provide a ton of value. And it wasn't until I took stock of all the things I had learned up to that point that I finally realized I *did* have something of value to offer: Over those first six deals, I had learned how to analyze deals, choose markets, hire property managers, and find contractors. I learned two different asset classes (long-term rentals and short-term rentals) and how to manage my investments remotely.

When I sat back and looked at all the things I had learned, I was able to let go of my imposter syndrome and tell myself that I was good enough to accept this amazing opportunity.

Why am I bringing this up?

As you've read through this chapter, some of you may have been wondering silently to yourself whether or not you even have anything of value to offer a potential partner. If you're feeling that way, I want you to stop and take note of all the things you've done in your investing journey so far. If you've already completed a few deals, then you should easily be able to rattle off the things that you had to do to get those deals closed.

If you're at zero, then ask yourself what some of your natural skills are (we'll touch on this more in the next section). Are you a good salesperson? Are you great with numbers? Are you handy? There are so many skills that people pick up outside of real estate investing that translate well to becoming a real estate investor.

At BPCon one year, Ashley and I hosted a small Q&A where someone told us they had no value to bring to a partnership. Ashley's first question was, "What is your current job?" He said he was a project manager at a tech company. Even though this isn't directly related to real estate or construction, there are so many useful aspects of that role that can translate into managing a rehab. We then asked the audience if any of them would benefit from having a partner with the skills and experience of being a project manager to oversee their rehabs. Hands went up across the room.

Even if you're coming up short on translatable skills, remember what I said about *capacity to learn*. Even if you feel you have nothing to add right now, do you believe in yourself enough to say, I can learn something of value?

Questions to Ask Yourself

We'll end this chapter with a little exercise to help you get your mind warmed up and thinking of ways you can add value. If you're like most people, you're probably great at identifying your weaknesses and where you need the help of others. Yet you probably struggle with being able to confidently say what you're good at and what kind of value you can bring to a partnership.

If that's true, then here are some questions you can ask yourself to identify what unique skills you can bring to a partnership.

Do I know any . . .
- Lenders or bankers?
- Property managers?
- Wholesalers?
- Realtors?
- Handymen or contractors?
- High net worth individuals?

Do I have the ability to . . .
- Research and identify potential markets?
- Analyze properties and determine if they're good deals?

- Manage people like property managers, housekeepers, contractors, and handymen?
- Create systems and processes to automate the business?
- Be an effective and persuasive salesperson?
- Set up and manage the software needed to run the business?
- Manage the books and keep the accounting in order?

Have I ever ...
- Purchased a home (investment property or otherwise)?
- Hired a property manager?
- Trained and onboarded an employee?
- Worked with lots of data?

Now that you're familiar with the Three Pillars of Partnership Value, hopefully you're able to identify both the value that you can bring to a partnership and the value that you'll need your partner to bring. With the value piece squared away, let's talk about how you can go about finding a partner who's a good fit for you.

REAL-LIFE PARTNERSHIPS
Vinci Sevilla Jr.
INVESTS IN: California, Arizona, West Virginia, Texas, Illinois, and Tennessee

My partner and I met each other in college, but it wasn't until eight years later that we reconnected when he liked a social media post of mine about buying a BiggerPockets book! We realized our mutual interest in real estate and liked the idea of investing together, so we decided to start out with a short-term rental partnership. Our partnership structure is 50/50, splitting the down payment, closing costs, and furnishing expenses. After the success of our first property, we continued expanding to more short-term rentals out of state! My strengths are operations, running numbers, and deal analysis. His strengths are in rehab, project management, and being our boots on the ground. Because of our partnership, we've both grown so much, and our families have become really close. On top of that, we continue to push and inspire each other in our journey toward financial freedom.

Chapter 3

HOW TO FIND A PARTNER

— Tony —

People do business with people they know, like, and trust. As you look for a partner—or in some cases, multiple partners—it becomes important for people to know, like, and trust *you*.

Think we're overstating this? Let's look at Airbnb as an illustration of why the principle of know, like, and trust (KLT) is so critical.

Airbnb: An Example of KLT

When you book a property on Airbnb, chances are you're staying at the home of a person you've never met before—which, when you think about it, is an odd thing. Under normal circumstances, you probably wouldn't feel safe or comfortable spending the night in a stranger's home.

So, what is it about booking through Airbnb that makes this less strange?

Airbnb has invested hundreds of millions of dollars into marketing with the goal of making you know, like, and trust Airbnb as a brand. Even if you don't personally know the owner of the property, you're comfortable booking their place because it's on a reputable site like Airbnb.

Defining KLT

Let's define each of these three words—know, like, and trust—as they relate to building your real estate business partnerships.

- **Know:** This means people are aware of who you are and what you're good at and that they've developed a relationship with you in some way. It's important for people to know you because you can't partner with someone you don't know. And the more people who know you, the bigger the pool of potential partners becomes.
- **Like:** This means that after people get to know you, they actually take pleasure in the relationship that's formed. They enjoy your company and associate your name with a positive feeling.
- **Trust:** Basically, this means that when you say something, people believe it to be true. If you say that you're going to do something, people believe that you'll follow through on it. It also means that people feel safe with you. And a feeling of safety is incredibly important for any partnership.

The relationship doesn't have to take shape in the traditional sense either. For example, when I listen to a podcast, I'm developing a relationship with the hosts and the guests on that podcast, even if I never meet them. And when I read a book, I develop a relationship with the author, even though I may have no idea what they look or sound like.

HOW TO BUILD "KNOW"

I started my first real estate investing podcast before I even closed on my first real estate deal. All I did on that podcast was interview people about their very first real estate investment. Why did I do this?

First, I have a passion for helping others, and a podcast seemed like a great way to realize that passion. Second, it was an easy way for me to build my network. I was interviewing dozens of investors, so I was constantly meeting people who were succeeding in an area that I aspired to succeed in. And at the same time, as the podcast grew, more and more listeners began to know who I was.

Basically, my podcast was an avenue for more people to know me. For example, I probably wouldn't be the host of the *Real Estate Rookie* podcast without that first podcast. The same goes with Ashley and her Instagram account. The producers would have no idea who we were, and we never would have been on their radar to audition for the positions. We were able to build the know, like, and trust from these platforms.

If starting a podcast or creating videos for social media isn't something you're comfortable with or any good at, then look for online communities where you can connect with people through your writing.

The BiggerPockets forums are *filled* with people who have found amazing business partners simply because one of those partners became well-known on the forums. You can set up keyword alerts that relate to your market or your type of real estate investing, and any time someone mentions those keywords in a post on the forum, you'll get a notification. From there, you can add value to that post and engage with other people on the topic.

For example, say you flip houses in Houston, Texas. You can set up an alert on the forums for "Houston" and "flipping." From there, any time anyone posts something about either house flipping or Houston, you'll get notified. Then you can go in and engage with people or answer questions they have about house flipping or the Houston market.

Over time, you could become the go-to person on the forums for house flipping in Houston. And now, whenever a member on the forums thinks of a house flipper or someone they know in the Houston market, you'll be the person they think of.

You can always go old-school and take it offline, too, by attending real estate events in person. Look up the local real estate meetup in your neighborhood and become a fixture at their events. Or, if you want to supercharge how many people know you, you can throw your own real estate meetup.

Imagine if you were the person who hosted the monthly local real estate meetup and you were able to get thirty, forty, or one hundred people into a room each month to talk about real estate. Even if you aren't the person getting up on the stage each month, just being the person who puts it all together will help you build your network and allow more people to know who you are.

HOW TO BUILD "LIKE"

Building "like" is a little more nuanced than "know." Just because someone knows who you are doesn't necessarily mean they like you. I'm sure we can all think of people we know yet don't like all that much.

Getting people to like you is not what I'm advocating; this isn't high school, and you aren't running for Prom Queen or King.

The truth is, some people are going to connect with you, and they're immediately going to be drawn into who you are. The two of you will just click. Maybe it's because you have similar backgrounds, upbringings, or interests. Whatever the reason, the person you are will resonate with some people.

On the flip side, some people *won't* connect with you, and it's not because you're a bad person. It could be because they have a different sense of humor or a different perspective on life.

You might be thinking, *If I have no control over whether or not people like me, what am I supposed to do at this step?* And the answer is . . .

Just be yourself.

That's it.

If you like quoting lines from funny movies, then do that. If you like making sports references, then do that. If you grew up on a farm in rural America, then share that. If you grew up in the middle of the biggest city in the world, then share that. The only way to win at this step is by being true to yourself and sharing that genuine version of yourself with everyone you meet. Over time, you'll naturally start to connect with people who know you *and* like you.

HOW TO BUILD TRUST

The final step of KLT is even more nuanced than the last. Trust, by its nature, is a delicate thing. It takes time to create and it's exceptionally fragile.

But the truth is, as more people get to know you, and those people end up liking you, those same people will naturally start to trust you as well.

One thing I've found that has helped build trust is to be honest about your mistakes. On the *Real Estate Rookie* podcast, both Ashley and I have shared mistakes and challenges we've made as we've built our businesses. (Note: Listen to Ashley's episode where her property tax bill wasn't paid, or Tony's episode where he talks about losing $30,000 on an investment!)

I think our listeners appreciate that honesty because oftentimes, people are too embarrassed to share their failures. But when you *do* share them, it helps people trust you more because it shows that you have nothing to hide.

Building a Platform

One of the ways to create massive amounts of KLT is by building a platform for yourself.

Have you noticed how someone with a lot of followers on social media is often seen as an expert? Let's say you see Instagram accounts for two chefs: One has 250,000 followers and one has 250 followers; which one would you rather have cook for you? Most likely you will pick the "famous" one. The person with only 250 followers might cook a more delicious meal, but they haven't put the time and energy into marketing themselves like the chef with 250,000 followers.

The more people who can attest to your credibility, the more you'll appeal to a potential partner. Unfortunately, having followers nowadays has somehow turned into a measure of credibility. Should that be the case? Probably not, but when you constantly talk about what you are doing, or trying to do, at some point you are seen as an expert. Is anyone fact-checking these social media influencers to know if what they are saying is true? Did they really make millions on a house flip? Can you really know? I'd like to assume most people aren't fabricating their financial success on their social media pages, but you shouldn't use this as a measure of whom you choose to invest with.

Still, in today's marketing, brand awareness—and who you know—holds a lot of power.

Ashley recently attended a virtual meetup hosted by AJ Osborne and Britt Arnason. An investor asked how he could present himself as credible to a lender and seller. He was trying to purchase a self-storage deal with bank financing and seller financing. Britt straight out told him to say he had AJ Osborne, "The Self-Storage King," as his advisor. Using the brand name of an expert carries weight.

Several years ago, Britt found her first self-storage deal. She needed $600,000 to purchase it. She told AJ, "There is no way someone would invest in self-storage with me. This is my first ever self-storage deal!" He said, "Well, just put it out there, and see what happens." If you don't know Britt, she has over 200,000 followers on Instagram, and after she posted in her story asking if anyone was interested in investing with her, she received over 300 email inquiries! That's a lot of people wanting to give her money to make them money. With so many people aware of her as a brand, Britt was able to quickly get a pool of potential investors.

Before you start panicking that you don't have a social media following or don't even use social media yet, don't worry—we've got you covered. Keep reading. We just wanted to give you a couple of examples of how presentation, marketing, your brand, and your pitch do play a role when you're seeking a partner. These things are especially important if you're pitching someone who isn't a close family member or friend but rather someone who knows nothing about you.

A question that inevitably comes up when we talk about building KLT is, Can I do this even if I'm a new investor? The answer is a resounding yes!

There's a misconception that getting people to know, like, and trust you as a real estate investor means you need to be wildly successful. But that's not true. Oftentimes, people gravitate toward others who are in situations similar to theirs, not necessarily to those who are ten or twenty steps ahead. Even if you're an aspiring investor who's completed zero deals, you can still use the principles in this chapter to build KLT.

You can still host that meetup. You can still start that podcast. You can still build your social media following. You can still contribute to the forums.

The only difference is that the focus of your content will be more on sharing your journey as opposed to trying to educate people. If you're up late analyzing a deal after you got off work, snap a picture and post that. If you're walking properties with your agent, record a video and share that. If you are in your property and replacing the floors, let people know that too.

The point is: Your journey is worth sharing. And that journey will help you build KLT, even if you're not an experienced investor. (Check out Lili Thompson, who started her YouTube channel before she even got her first deal. She documented her journey to that first deal and still documents her progress today as she continues to grow her portfolio.)

The Magic of Initiating Conversations

We started the section on finding a partner with the KLT concept because once you master this, it becomes exponentially easier to find the right people to partner with in your real estate business. You'll have a larger pool of people to choose from, and you can give yourself the best odds of finding the *right* partner instead of settling for the *first* partner.

My first real estate partnership came from an unlikely source.

I was scrolling through Instagram and saw a post by David Greene (cohost of the *BiggerPockets Real Estate* podcast) and I clicked through to David's profile. Using Instagram's feature of showing yours and another profile's mutual followers, I looked through ours, seeing several names I expected before one that caught my eye.

That person was my wife's cousin. At that time, he was more of a distant relative, and I had only met him a few times in all the years my wife and I had been together. But I was so surprised to see his name as a mutual follower because I had no idea that he was also interested in real estate.

A few months passed and I ended up seeing him at a family party, and I brought up how I stumbled across his profile on Instagram. We ended up chatting a bit about how he had been thinking about investing in real estate, and I shared that I had been thinking the same thing. We spent some time just trading notes and talking shop. Nothing earth-shattering happened during that conversation. We shook hands and went our separate ways.

Over the next few months, he and I kept in touch, talking every so often. One night, I ended up getting an offer accepted on a property for which I needed a partner. I sent the deal out to a few people in my network, and he was the first to respond saying he was ready to go. Below is a screenshot of the actual email I sent. I also included a copy of the BiggerPockets Calculator report that showed my analysis of the property along with a few rental comps.

And that was the start of our partnership. Today, we own a thriving real estate business together and it all started with me stumbling across his profile on social media.

Why do I share this story? Because it's important for you to understand something: There may be people in your network *right now* who have an interest in investing in real estate but haven't openly expressed that to you. And the only way you'll find those people who have secret dreams of investing in real estate is if *you* initiate that conversation.

Let's get into the nitty-gritty here about actually finding that partner.

Creating a Potential Partner List

The first exercise is to think through your current network and create a list of anyone and everyone you think might be interested in partnering with you.

Maybe they've mentioned to you in the past that they've always thought about investing. Or maybe they posted a copy of the real estate book they were reading on social media. Or, like me, maybe they follow BiggerPockets on social media.

Think about current and previous coworkers, old classmates, family, friends, people you follow on social media, people who go to your gym or are part of the same clubs you belong to, and literally anyone else you can think of who may be even slightly interested in real estate investing.

When You Don't Have a List

For some of you reading this, you might not be able to come up with any names in your network. Maybe everyone you know right now has zero interest in investing in real estate (or if they do, they've never mentioned it to you before). If this is the case for you, don't freak out. This is totally normal, especially for new investors.

When I first started my real estate investing journey, it felt lonely. I was reading all of these books, listening to all of these podcasts, and watching all of these YouTube videos, and I literally had no one to talk to about everything I was learning.

One of the benefits of living in the 21st century is that the entire world is connected. You can be sitting in your bedroom and have a conversation with someone clear on the other side of the globe. Leverage that connectivity to help you find your potential partners. Here are some ways to do this:

- **Create a profile on BiggerPockets** and post an introduction so people can get to know you. BiggerPockets is literally the world's largest online forum solely dedicated to real estate investing. There's a tremendous opportunity to find and connect with other people on that platform.

- **Join at least one Facebook group** that's focused on investing in real estate. There are countless groups on Facebook that deal with real estate investing. Find one that resonates with you, and get active by introducing yourself and adding value where you can.

- **Find at least one local real estate meetup** and RSVP for the next event. Going offline and meeting face-to-face is one of the best and easiest ways to get to know new people. Everyone who comes to the meetup is there to network and make new connections, so it's the perfect place for a new investor to build relationships.

- **Purchase a ticket to at least one real estate conference** this year. Aside from the actual learning that takes place at conferences, the networking is some of the best you'll find. Conferences, in my opinion, are one step above free meetups for networking because the level of commitment of people at conferences is typically higher than at the local meetup—simply because you have to pay to attend. And if someone is ready to spend a few hundred bucks on a ticket, plus the cost of a flight and hotel, plus taking time off work, then they'll probably be serious about getting started as an investor.

What to Do with Your List

Once you've created your list of potential partners, it's time to start reaching out to them!

At this point, the purpose of reaching out to them is *not* to start the partnership. The only reason you're reaching out is to understand if they're even interested in investing in real estate.

After you establish that there's an interest, you can start progressing down the path to creating a partnership.

Remember my story of how I found my first partner; it was a casual conversation. I just brought up the fact that I saw his name as someone who followed an influential real estate investor, and the conversation flowed from there.

As you're reaching out to these people on your list, try saying something as simple as:

- "Are you still thinking about investing in real estate?"
- "There's a real estate meetup happening this week. Wanna go together?"
- "I saw your post about reading that real estate investing book—are you looking to get started?"
- "I know you've talked about quitting your job one day . . . have you thought about real estate investing?"

The options are endless, but the point here is just to gauge this person's interest in investing in real estate. This removes the chance that either you or the other person might feel pressured by the idea of rushing into an actual partnership.

Brandon Turner, an author, entrepreneur, and real estate investor, once gave Ashley the advice of not directly asking a potential partner straight out for capital or to be partners. He said one way you can avoid the awkwardness and possible confrontation is to ask the person indirectly. Ashley likes to avoid confrontation at all costs (hence why she has a partner who's good at handling this!), so this little trick from Brandon has helped her.

Brandon suggested approaching the person you want to ask and saying, "Do you know anyone who would be _____ ?" Insert your question here. Some examples: "Do you know anyone who would be interested in partnering on a rental property?" "Do you know anyone who would be interested in lending private money?"

This takes the pressure off asking the person directly. It gives them a chance to think, and they don't feel confronted. It plants the seed that they may be interested themselves and don't want to pass up the opportunity you may be providing! Also, if they know someone, it gives them the opportunity to refer that person.

The Importance of Vetting

A smart investor or potential partner will want to vet you. They won't go off your word or your Instagram posts.

There will be some people, though, who don't want to verify anything. But if the person is someone you don't know, and they are super eager to jump into a partnership with you, that might be a red flag. What else are they overeager to jump into?

If you know the person and have already built trust, then it could be a different story as to why they don't want to fact-check you.

I have an investor friend, Tyler, who uses a lot of private money lenders. These lenders don't have equity or control over the deal, and it's not a true partnership where they are tied together past that one deal. Tyler has told me that he's never had a private money lender ask for any of the information I went over above. Can you believe that? People just inherently trust him, hear about the opportunity through word of mouth, and want to invest! Tyler does send out an investment packet to each private money lender outlining the deal and some track record of the previous deals that Tyler has completed with his partner. Still, the lenders never want to fact-check Tyler or his partner and their credibility or financial stability.

Think about the type of person you want as your partner. How are they vetting you? This is something to be cautious about as you vet them in turn. Yes, you want them to trust you right off the bat, but do you want them to trust *everyone* right away? Do you want a partner who is overly cautious, only making decisions or commitments after first going through a series of verifications and getting the data? There is a fine line here, though—you don't want them to be overly critical and focusing on minutiae, which can turn into just nitpicking and being petty.

"Date" Before You "Marry"

Imagine that you're single, and you're going on a date with someone for the first time. You do the usual dinner and movie, and you have the time of your life. The night is filled with laughter and deep talks and time flies because you enjoyed yourself so much. Now imagine if at the end of the date instead of that person leaning in for a good-night kiss, they leaned in and asked, "Will you marry me?"

Most people reading this book would probably say no in this scenario. Honestly, they'd probably be slightly concerned that this other person wanted to move so fast, and it might end the relationship altogether.

Why is that?

Just because you had one amazing date with someone doesn't mean you'll have an amazing life with them. There are still so many questions you'll need to ask and so many stones that will need to be turned before you feel comfortable committing your life to this one person.

Your real estate partnerships are the same way. It's best to "date" for a while before you commit to building a full-blown partnership with one another.

Before my partner and I started our company, we did a single deal together. And before that single deal, we chatted and met several times. Prior to launching our business, we already had the experience of working together. We knew we liked each other and that our skill sets and personalities meshed well. And before doing that first deal, we were really just trying to make sure that we could get along and that our long-term goals were the same.

It's in both yours and your potential partner's best interest to take it slow and "date" before you jump into a partnership. Below are a few ways you can help build that relationship before officially entering into a partnership.

- **Get aligned on your goals.** This is a crucial step. We'll touch more on this in Chapter 5, but getting clarity on what you're both working toward—and what you want from the real estate business and the partnership—is critical for the success of the partnership.
- **Take a personality test.** It's also helpful to take a personality test so you can better understand one another, as I discussed in Chapter 2. My partner and I took both the Myers-Briggs and DISC profile tests for this reason. And we realized through those tests that we had complementary personality types. It also helped us understand the different perspectives that each of us has when it comes to life and business. I prefer structure; he prefers fluidity. I'm more of a visionary; he's more of a tactician. These are differences that are sometimes hard to recognize without the help of a personality test.
- **Analyze deals together.** This one is a bit more tactical but also extremely helpful. I did this early on in my partnership, and it helped us get clarity on the types of properties we wanted to purchase. I would send a deal to my partner, and he'd point out what he did and didn't like about the deal. He would also send me deals, and I'd give him my feedback. That back-and-forth helped us in two ways: First, it forced us to clarify the type of properties we wanted to buy. Second, it made us have a discussion to make sure we were aligned on the type of properties we wanted to buy. It's a smart idea to start analyzing deals together *before* you actually buy a property.

Now that we've discussed how to find a partner, it's time for the next step: how to present yourself to your potential partner.

REAL-LIFE PARTNERSHIPS
Jessie Dillon
INVESTS IN: Massachusetts, New Hampshire, and Illinois

After buying my first three turnkey buy-and-hold properties in an expensive market in just nine months, I was tapped out of down payment money. While it wasn't a shock, and I was super happy with my investments, I still felt like I must have screwed up somewhere along the way to be freshly out of funds! Saving my way to another $75,000 felt impossible at the time, so I was at a standstill, becoming more frustrated and less confident every day. Then I went to BPCon for the first time and realized in my conversations that, for one reason or another, everyone hits a point where investing needs to become a team sport if they want to keep going. What I thought was a roadblock was really a rite of passage.

I'd been resistant to partnerships because I've been self-employed since 2017; I don't like a lot of hands in the pot! But BPCon helped me see that while I have time and knowledge, I lack funds. Meanwhile, there are a ton of people who have funds but lack time and knowledge! It took me a few weeks to put my imposter syndrome aside and start tapping into my network.

I'm so glad I did, because I was quickly introduced to my ideal partners, and we're about to close on a thirteen-unit property out of state. She brings the down payment, closing costs, and working capital to the deal, and I do the rest. We'll be splitting cash flow and ownership 50/50, with a plan to hold the property for at least five years. We operate and close under a trust that's owned 50/50 by my and my partner's LLCs.

What makes our partnership ideal is that we have similar financial goals, we communicate effectively, and she has total faith in me as an operator. Three more deals like this one will set me up for life, and going forward, even when I no longer need access to start-up funding, I'd prefer to keep working with partners. Real estate really is more fun and less scary when you're not in it alone!

Chapter 4
PARTNER PRESENTATION

— Ashley —

Your ability to find the right partner is directly related to your ability to communicate the value that you bring to the partnership.

In fact, you'll want to overwhelm your potential partner with this information. There is nothing better than being prepared to answer every question or provide visualization or proof to support what you're saying.

In order to put together a solid presentation that conveys your value to your potential partner, you'll need to address three main elements:

- Your experience and skill set
- Your financial foundation
- Your business plan, either with or without a deal analysis

Let's go over each element in detail.

Experience and Skill Set

We've mentioned this already, but it's worth repeating: Your experience doesn't necessarily have to be tied to real estate investing. You've probably acquired experience and developed skills in different aspects of your life that may be of significant value for a potential real estate partnership.

There are many skill sets that aren't directly related to real estate that can be advantageous; maybe you currently work in customer service and want to do short-term rentals. Managing short-term rentals means you are now in the hospitality industry, which is largely customer service–based. Having the knowledge, patience, and skill set to effectively and properly handle your guests is an asset. On the other hand, maybe you're a bookkeeper or an accountant, which enables you to easily keep records of transactions and manage the money.

Don't limit your current capabilities. If it helps, write out a list of your skills. Even if you dislike your current job, there is surely at least one skill you've learned in that position that you can take advantage of as an investor.

CASE STUDY

If you've built a real estate portfolio or have a track record of investing in real estate, then use that as your case study. Use that as proof that you know what you're doing. One deal is more experience than most people have!

I am often asked, How do I get my spouse on board? My best piece of advice for that situation is to show them. Create a visual. I am not saying to draw the house you want to buy, but lay out the numbers for your spouse. The same principle applies to a business partnership. You can verbally walk them through the numbers on your recent deals, but putting it all on paper and making it visual can create a greater impact.

The following documents can help you show the results of the deal (or deals) you have completed:

- Profit and loss statement for the current year to date or the previous year

- BiggerPockets Calculator Report (or comparable deal-analysis tool)
- Excel sheet or your own calculator analysis that you use to analyze deals

Financial Foundation

After you have wowed your potential partner with your experience and skill set, show them that you are not only successful in business, but in your own personal finances as well. Rest assured, it doesn't matter how much money you have; what matters is how you manage the money you *do* have.

Documentation that shows your financial responsibility might include:

- **Personal Financial Statement**

  This statement shows your assets minus your liabilities, which equals your net worth. An "asset" is defined as property owned by a person and is considered to have worth or value. A "liability" is a responsibility you have to another, usually as a financial obligation. Examples of assets are cash under your mattress, cash in checking or savings accounts, retirement accounts, investment accounts, vehicles, jewelry, real estate, and collectibles. Examples of liabilities are any type of loan: a mortgage, a car loan, money owed to a friend or family member. If you are unsure how to even start a personal financial statement, we recommend downloading an app called Personal Capital. You can link your accounts to automatically pull the information to show your net worth.

PERSONAL FINANCIAL STATEMENT TEMPLATE

ASSETS	ACCOUNT NUMBER	CASH OR MARKET VALUE
Cash		
Checking Account		
Savings Account		
Other:		
Other:		
Other:		
Other:		
Retirement Accounts		
401K		
IRA		
Certificate of Deposit		
Bonds		
Stock Options		
Trust Account		
Cash Value of Life Insurance		
Mutual Fund		
Stocks		
Money Market		
TOTAL:		

OTHER ASSETS

Accounts Receivable		
Business Equity		
Vehicles		
Jewelry		

Household Furnishings		
Other:		
Other:		
Other:		
TOTAL:		

REAL ESTATE ASSETS

Primary Residence		
Investment Property		
Other:		
Other:		
TOTAL:		
TOTAL ASSETS:		

LIABILITIES	ACCOUNT NUMBER	CURRENT BALANCE
Primary Mortgage		
Investment Property Mortgage		
Line of Credit		
Credit Card		
Car Loan		
Student Loan		
Other Loan or Debts:		
Other Loan or Debts:		

TOTAL LIABILITIES:

NET WORTH = (ASSETS - LIABILITIES)

- **Credit Report**

  Your credit report shows debt you have acquired and your repayment history. A score is created based on multiple factors, including your amount of debt, your credit usage, how often your credit is pulled, and timely payments. There are free websites where you can see an estimate of your credit score. This estimate can be quite different from what the actual credit reporting agents have as your score, but the advantage to having it is that you can see the activity on your credit report; get alerts when your credit is pulled, if you have high usage, and if you miss a payment; and just track how different factors affect your credit. If you have poor credit, you need to start working on correcting it. Every twelve months you can pull your actual credit by going to annualcreditreport.com, and it won't count against you. A partner will want to know that you're responsible with your own money and that you will be responsible with the money you invest together, and a high credit score will help demonstrate this.

- **Personal Tax Return**

  This one isn't as important as the other two. A tax return shows how much money you are currently making, but you can show that on the profit and loss statement. It also doesn't show what you do with the money you currently have. Still, you can't have too much information to give a potential investor, especially if it's beneficial information. I once had someone tell me they didn't want to give their personal information such as their tax return with their social security number on it, in case the person stole their identity. The first thing I'll say is if you're already leery of this person stealing your identity, then you probably shouldn't be investing with them. Secondly, you can easily cross or cut out your social security number or account information on documents. If you do have a current partnership and file a partnership return, then you could also include that tax return.

- **Credit Reference Letter**

  Another supporting document you could provide is a credit reference letter. If you have taken out a loan from a local lender or a private lender, even if it's a friend or family member, you can ask them for a letter stating your history with them. You can ask them to write about your timely payments and being easy to work with when you initially applied for your loan. You can also provide a sample template letter for them with the understanding that it can be altered as needed, but it at least starts the process for them. Here's a sample letter:

October 12, 2023

To Whom It May Concern:

Daryl Clinch has been a customer of HG Bank for seven years. Over that time, Mr. Clinch has taken out one residential loan and two commercial loans. Each loan payment for all three loans has been completed in a timely manner. Mr. Clinch has never acquired a late fee on any of his accounts. Mr. Clinch has opened a checking and savings account with us, and all are in good standing. HG Bank appreciates Mr. Clinch as a customer and would like to continue that relationship with further opportunities.

Thank you,
Dan Puffer
Loan Officer
HG Bank

BOOKKEEPING

If you don't have proper bookkeeping for your current deals, whether a flip, long-term rental, or any other strategy, then you are not building a strong foundation. You must have certain fundamentals, and good recordkeeping is one of them, whether you do it yourself or outsource it. If you need help doing it yourself, look into software such as Stessa, QuickBooks, or property management software with bookkeeping integration (RentRedi or Buildium are two of many that I've tested). There are also affordable virtual assistants on websites like Upwork that can assist you in getting your books cleaned up and completing your monthly bookkeeping.

Business Plan

Along with proving yourself to potential partners, you need to showcase your deal, or at least provide your specific goals. It's exciting to talk about an idea you have and all the money you can make, but do you know how many people simply dream and don't make a concrete plan? Tarl Yarber, CEO and founder of a leading investment company in the Pacific Northwest, once said to me, "You wouldn't hire a builder who simply had a dream of building your home. You'd hire a builder who had a plan as to how to build your home."

The best way to show preparedness is to have a written business plan. What's your investment strategy? What's your buying criteria? What's your analysis on the property you want to purchase? You want all of this to be very clear to your partner up front, not just later on when your business is already in motion.

A business plan starts with an overview of your business and should answer the following questions:

- What does your business do?
- How will your business make money?
- What services or products will be sold?
- What are the expected processes?
- What is your marketing plan?
- Who is your competition?
- What are your financial projections and capital needs?

BUSINESS PLAN TEMPLATE

Company Name:

Identity	Problem
Our solution	Target market
The competition	Revenue streams
Marketing activities	Expenses
Team and key roles	Milestones

The Deal

If you already have a deal picked out, this is where the fun part comes in. As part of your business plan, you can show your potential partner the exact property you have in mind and how the numbers will work out.

We recommend using the BiggerPockets Calculator report (www.biggerpockets.com/calculators) or an alternate deal analysis tool as long as it's user-friendly, meaning that someone who doesn't have knowledge in real estate or experience with analyzing a deal can easily read and interpret the report.

There is no point in overcomplicating the analysis. You can make it simple and still include all of the pertinent information.

Let's go through an example for a rental property deal you would like to purchase. Your analysis should include the following details:

Property Address

Provide the location of the property. You can also include some information about that market and explain why it would be a good idea to invest in this area. You can take it a step further and include a market analysis of the area too.

Start off by listing the industries that offer job opportunities in this area, which showcases where your tenants will come from. If there are jobs, people will need housing. Include any attractive amenities in the area such as parks, a highly rated school district, shops and restaurants, and other attractions that may draw people to the area.

Then pull some statistics on the area showing population growth, average income of renters, average home value, and the average sale price. This will give your potential partner an idea of what the market conditions are like and how good your deal is within that market.

It's easy to say a property costs $50,000 and rents for $1,000 with no rehab. Wow, that looks like a great deal! However, perhaps the property is in a high-crime neighborhood, and the house has already had the AC unit stolen three times in the past year. Replacing the AC unit could eat up your cash flow in no time, making it not such a great deal after all.

Property Description

What type of property is it? How many units? How many bedrooms and bathrooms? What are some positives about the property? What needs to be fixed on the property? Is there any value that could be added to the property?

Purchase Price

What is the price you're offering to pay for the property? How will you pay for the property? Cash from each investor, a mortgage, or private money? If there will be debt on the property, include the terms of that debt, such as interest rate and amortization.

Closing Costs, Rehab Costs, and Start-up Costs

What will need to be paid for when acquiring the property, and how will it be paid?

Income

What will the rent be for each unit of this property? Also, be sure to include any additional income streams like parking, laundry, or other services that tenants might pay for.

Expenses

What expenses will the property incur? There will be variable expenses in addition to fixed expenses.

Variable expenses will fluctuate from month to month and can be difficult to estimate. It is common to use a percentage of the revenue to estimate these expenses. The main examples of these include vacancy (when you don't have any rent coming in and need to cover expenses those months), capital expenditures (repairs or maintenance that are improvements to the property and need to be depreciated, such as a new roof), and repairs and maintenance (general repairs that randomly come up, including fixing a leaking faucet or a heating element in a hot water tank).

Fixed expenses, on the other hand, are usually steady each month: utilities, lawn care and/or snow removal, insurance, property taxes, garbage removal, HOA fees, mortgage payment, and management fees.

Estimating your expenses can be a bit tricky, but by doing some internet research, you'll find what you can expect to pay for utilities, insurance, and basic repairs and expenses. One of the best ways to get solid numbers on expenses is to reach out to existing investors in that market and ask them what they're paying in expenses.

The Outcome

After collecting the income and paying the fixed and estimated variable expenses each month, how much money is left for cash flow?

METHODS TO EVALUATE A DEAL

There are several methods for evaluating properties, and it would be a good idea to include a few of them in your analysis. You should never rely solely on one type of evaluation.

Let's look at some of the different methods we can use to evaluate a real estate deal.

Cash-on-Cash Return

To calculate your cash-on-cash return (expressed as a percentage), take your annual cash flow and divide it by the total amount of cash that was invested into the deal. This cash includes your down payment, closing costs, rehab costs, and any other start-up costs associated with getting the property "rent ready." You can calculate your cash-on-cash return on an individual basis or as a total for all partners.

For example, let's say Remington invests $20,000 into a deal for 50 percent equity in the property. The property cash flows $6,000 that year. Remington's percentage of the cash flow is $3,000 ($6,000 × 50%). $3,000/$20,000 = 15% cash-on-cash return.

One Percent Rule

The 1 percent rule states that the monthly rent charged should be at least 1 percent of the purchase price. This is referred to as the price-to-rent ratio. Before you gauge if the 1 percent rule is a feasible measurement, you should study your market and see what the average price-to-rent ratio is. In more expensive markets, hitting the 1 percent rule can prove to be difficult. However, it's important to point out that just because a property fails the 1 percent rule doesn't automatically mean it's a bad deal.

For example, you could still be cash flow positive on a property that doesn't meet the 1 percent rule, but once you add in appreciation and depreciation, it could be an amazing deal. In less expensive markets, like Buffalo, New York, it's extremely easy to hit the 1 percent. But remember, the 1 percent rule is just one measure, and while it's easy to hit the 1 percent rule in less expensive markets, it could be increasingly difficult to hit the next "rule."

Fifty Percent Rule

This rule states that your expenses should total no more than 50 percent of your rental income. In Buffalo, it is more difficult to hit this rule because the property taxes are so high, and therefore your expenses are much higher.

Once again, you need to gauge your market before using this measurement to decide what is a good deal or not. Because of this, your analysis should include the typical price-to-rent ratios and expense ratios for that market.

Purchase Cap Rate

The purchase cap rate is more commonly used in commercial real estate investments as a measurement. This is calculated by taking the net operating income (not including the mortgage principal and interest payment) and dividing it by the market value of the property.

Return on Investment

The last measurement you can include is the return on investment (ROI). This is a projected number; you don't know what the ROI is since the property has not performed yet. The ROI is calculated by taking the net return on investment and dividing it by the cost of the investment multiplied by 100 percent.

PROPERTY PHOTOS

Along with providing the deal analysis, include pictures of the property. These could be from the MLS, provided by a wholesaler, or pictures you took yourself. Give your potential partner a visual of what kind of property you are looking at. If the property needs to be rehabbed, then provide your potential partner with a detailed scope of work. If this is something you need their help with, then give the information you do know. This goes for all aspects of your deal analysis.

If you don't know for certain, don't BS it. Be honest. Do you recall the pyramid at the beginning of the book? Communication was at the top. Fill in what information you do know. For the rehab, if you already know some obvious repairs that need to be done, list those initially without a cost associated with it if you don't know. That's where you will let your partner provide value or you will have a plan in place to get estimates to figure out those costs.

SAMPLE SCOPE OF WORK

Here is a sample scope of work that you can use as a template:

■ *The work shall include, but not be limited to, all labor, materials, tools, equipment, incidentals, insurance, overhead, and profit to perform the work as outlined below:*
■ *Materials will be purchased with Colt + Farmhouse Development LLC credit card*

1. Demolition   **$500**
   Scope Items
    1. **Kitchen Demolition**
       a. Remove cabinets and countertops
       b. Remove appliances
       c. Remove wall paneling
    2. **Master Bedroom Demolition**
       a. Remove carpet and curtains
       b. Remove heater from wall
    3. **Main Floor Bathroom Demolition**
       a. Remove shower, cabinet, hot water heater, toilet, and vanity
    4. **Basement Demolition**
    5. **Living Room Demolition**
       a. Remove metal from around wood stove
    6. **Entry Way Demolition**
       a. Remove ceiling
       b. Remove entry door and storm door

7. **Upstairs Loft**
   a. Remove half wall in loft
8. **Miscellaneous Demo Items**
   a. Remove garbage and debris from all levels
   b. Remove pull-down ladder to loft
   c. Remove ceiling from basement

2. Landscaping, Decking, and Curb Appeal $6,000
   Scope Items
   1. Remove decking at entry and side of house and build new deck that wraps around entry room
   2. Flower beds around entry
   3. Firepit with gravel

3. Exterior Doors & Windows $3,800
   Scope Items
   1. **Door**
      a. Remove existing entry door and replace with new entry storm door at front entrance
   2. **Windows**
      a. Remove and replace (9) windows
   3. **Miscellaneous Items**
      a. Install caulking, flashing, trim boards around doors, windows to provide watertight installation as needed

4. Roof $5,000
   Scope Items
   1. Install metal roof over existing roof
   2. Add new soffit and gutters around edge of roof

5. Siding
   Scope Items
   1. Power wash siding and stain shaker shingles

6. Interior Drywall/Framing/Insulation $500
Scope Items
1. **Kitchen Scope of Work**
   a. Install insulation and drywall in kitchen
2. **Bathroom Scope of Work**
   a. Construct new shower niche
   b. Frame out closet for hot water heater
   c. Install ceiling and wall drywall
   d. Install HardieBacker board for floors and shower
3. **Miscellaneous Items**
   a. Skim coating walls as required where wall covering is removed
   b. Patching/wall prep of miscellaneous cracks in walls/ceilings
   c. Patching/wall prep of miscellaneous holes in walls/ceilings
   d. Install shoe molding and transition moldings as needed for laminate flooring install

7. Cabinetry Install $2,500
Scope Items
1. **Kitchen**
   a. Install kitchen cabinets per the layout shown
   b. Install kitchen cabinets: base, upper, and lower
   c. Install filler panels, end panels, and trim pieces
   d. Install cabinet door pulls
2. **Bathrooms**
   a. Install new vanity cabinet
3. **Miscellaneous Items**
   a. Provide all necessary shims and fasteners as required
   b. Butcher-block countertop

8. Interior Doors & Trim Install
Scope Items
1. **Doors**
   a. Install all new six-panel doors in bedroom and bathroom
   b. Install all new door latches and handles
2. **Trim & Woodwork**
   a. Install wooden stairs to loft
   b. Install trim along floor after luxury vinyl plank (LVP) and tile installed

9. Flooring $2,000
1. Install LVP in entry, living room, and lower bedroom
2. Sand upstairs wood floor and polyurethane
3. Install tile flooring in kitchen, bathroom, and dining area

10. Tiling $2,000
Scope Items
1. **Bathroom**
   a. Install floor tile in standard floor tile pattern on bathroom floor
   b. Install wall shower tile above basin
2. **Kitchen**
   a. Install tile backsplash in kitchen below kitchen cabinets
   b. Install tile floor in kitchen
3. **Dining area**
   a. Install tile floor same as kitchen and bathroom
4. **Miscellaneous**
   a. Install HardieBacker or cement board (contractor's preference) at all tile areas
   b. Install all grout

11. Interior Painting $250
Scope Items
1. Paint exposed drywall in bathroom and kitchen

12. Appliances $1,500
Scope Items
1. **Install and connect owner-furnished kitchen appliances**
   a. Apartment-sized range (electric)
   b. Apartment-sized fridge
   c. Countertop dishwasher
   d. All cords, hoses, and connections to be installed
   e. Microwave hood with exhaust

13. Plumbing $2,500
Scope Items
1. Remove any existing piping as required to complete new plumbing work
2. **Kitchen**
   a. Install water supply and new waste lines to sink
   Note: Sink to be installed by countertop installation contractor
   b. Install new kitchen faucet
3. **Bathroom**
   a. Install water supply and waste lines for new toilet, shower, vanity sink, and faucet
   b. Install new plumbing fixtures
      i. Toilet
      ii. Showerhead kit
      iii. Vanity sink and faucet
   c. Tankless hot water heater installed in bathroom

14. HVAC $2,500
Scope Items
1. Install Mitsubishi split unit in bedroom (AC and heat)

15. Electrical $1,500
Scope Items
1. Replace all existing outlets w/ new white outlets
2. Install new breaker box

3. Kitchen
   a. Install new GFI-protected outlets along new kitchen cabinet layout as required by code
   b. Install new outlets for appliances as required
   c. Install new light fixture
4. Main Level Bathroom
   a. Install new GFI-protected outlet at vanity cabinet
   b. Install exhaust fan with light
5. Existing Light Fixtures
   a. Replace all existing light fixtures with new ones provided

16. Upstairs Loft $2,000
   1. Remove existing half wall and replace with railing
   2. Install wooden staircase into loft

17. Miscellaneous Items $250
Scope Items
   1. Install bath accessories (toilet paper bar, towel bar)
   2. Install bathroom mirror

Total Rehab Budget: $32,800.00

As your deal progresses, you will probably revise and add more detail, but this is a good starting point to give your potential partner an overall idea of what the rehab will consist of. If you already have quotes and estimates for the repairs, include those in the deal analysis as well.

If you have no idea how to even start figuring out the estimated cost for a rehab, then simply start with the materials. Pick a room in the house and go one room at a time.

Let's use the bathroom as an example. You want to remodel the half bathroom. The drywall can stay, but you are going to demo the flooring, toilet, and vanity. Watch a YouTube video on what materials you need to install a tile floor. It should say something along the lines of "tile for XX amount of square feet, grout, spacers, thin-set to hold the tiles in place, and sponges."

You will then take this information and input it into a spreadsheet such as Excel, and pull up your favorite hardware website to start searching for each product. Next, write the associated cost next to each product, which gives you an idea of what your material costs will be. Also include a link to the webpage for each product, so if you do end up needing to order more materials, you'll have it all in one place for easy ordering.

Tip: Home Depot offers a bid room option when buying in bulk. Speak to your local Home Depot commercial services representative to request the email for their bid room. For the bid room, you send in a list of materials you need to order, and they will send back a discounted cost for all the materials.

In Sum: The Presentation

The three main components to your partnership presentation include your experience and skill set, your financial foundation, and your business plan, either with or without a deal analysis. These core items will give a potential partner the information they need up front to evaluate the opportunity you have for them. They may not have even considered asking for some of this information. Often people are either eager to jump at an opportunity or hesitant to take that step. You want to be prepared for both situations.

Before we further discuss building the partnership, let's go into more detail on making sure that your partner is aligned with your goals. Creating alignment on a single deal is easy, but we want to show you how to create alignment for the long haul.

Chapter 5

GOAL ALIGNMENT

— *Ashley* —

Everyone can start at the same spot, but that doesn't mean they will travel the same path, make the same pit stops, or reach the same place. To arrive at your destination, you need to have a desire, a goal, or something to achieve.

Chances are you've set goals before, in your personal life, career, or business. Maybe it was a fitness goal, an academic goal of getting an A on a test, or desiring a promotion at work. Similarly, in real estate investing, there needs to be a goal you aim to achieve.

Before we talk about goal setting with a partner and what that alignment looks like, let's focus on figuring out what your own specific goals are.

What Is a Goal?

A goal is a desired end state. It's the thing you want to achieve that requires ambition and effort to realize. It's the result that brings you joy. Setting and achieving goals are what make life exciting and allow you to live the life you've always dreamed of living.

Think of building a house. You have a particular vision or dream of what it will look like. You can picture the hickory kitchen cabinets, the white granite countertops, the master closet with custom drawers and shelving, and the well-manicured lawn that adds to the curb appeal.

Awesome. You have the first step, the vision. Now how do you actually get that house?

This is where you break down your goal even further. Think about what your biggest obstacle is at that very moment to building and moving into that dream house. As an example, let's use the most common obstacle: You don't have the money to afford it.

Next, break down how much money you'll need to reach your goal. You'll need to find out how much the house would cost to build, or at least get an estimate. How much money would you need for the down payment? How much money would you need in order to afford the monthly mortgage payment? Or, are you able to pay for the house in cash?

Then you'll need to figure out how you're going to get the money you need and so on in order to achieve your goal.

We'll cover breaking down your goal into specific, actionable tasks, but first let's talk more about what kind of goals you want to set.

S.M.A.R.T. Goals

Whatever your goal is, you'll want it to be a S.M.A.R.T. goal. This acronym describes the basic characteristics that a goal should have in order to lead you to a higher success rate in reaching it.

- **Specific**
  You have narrowed down and defined the details of what you want. The goal is not general.
- **Measurable**
  There is a specific way to measure if you have reached your goal. For example, a goal that isn't measurable would be: "I want to make money to build a house." A measurable goal would be: "I want to save $80,000 and reach $10,000 a month in passive income."

- **Attainable**

  If you are currently making $3,500 a month, and in the next three years you want to make $10 million and build your $20 million dream home overlooking the ocean, your goal may not be realistic. The goal should push you but not be exaggerated to the point where you don't even feel motivated to reach it because it just seems so far-fetched.

- **Relevant**

  Think about why you are setting this goal. Is it actually something you want? It should be something that aligns with what you are currently doing.

- **Time Bound**

  There should be a time frame as to when the goal will be completed. This will help you stay on track and keep you accountable to your goal. For all you procrastinators, knowing a deadline is approaching may be the little extra push that you need. Your time frame should also be realistic. It shouldn't be so far away that it seems like it's never going to happen, nor should it be too close to a constraint that makes it impossible to reach.

Defining Success Your Way

Let's face it, not everyone views success the same way. Your 21-year-old brother in college may view an undefeated run in beer pong as his success for the week. Your mom may get a job promotion, which feels like success to her. Your uncle may get a twelve-point buck during hunting season, and that could be his success story of the year. Your cousin's daughter could be admitted to the elite preschool of their choice, and that's your cousin's idea of success.

There are so many different measures of success, but no one else can decide what success means for you. In school, you were probably taught that good grades meant success or that job promotions mean you're achieving success. While that could be what you want, it's not for everyone.

You'll need to figure out what motivates and pushes *you* to reach your version of success. Start by defining what success looks like to you. Is it time freedom? Being able to drive your kids to school every day? Earning $1 million in a year? Buying a mansion on the beach or a cabin deep in the forest, off the grid? The options are endless. *Whatever you want.* If you don't try to get what you want, you'll never even get close to it, and honestly, sometimes it's the journey that ends up being the best part.

Goal Alignment with Your Partner

Once you have identified your goal or idea of success, you need to discuss this with your potential partner(s). It's extremely important to make sure your long-term goals align.

Do you want a massive business with an office and fifty employees? Does your partner want a lifestyle business that allows her to work from anywhere? If your goals don't align, then you'll inevitably have friction as the business grows. If your business isn't going to help you reach your goal, what's the point? Is it just to make money? Will that money help you reach your goal or ultimately pull you further away by becoming a huge time commitment?

The opportunities that can arise from partnerships are never-ending, but they can get out of control if there aren't clear expectations.

Let's go through an example. One situation that may arise is a conflict of time commitment expectations, which could affect your goal. Perhaps you want time freedom and suddenly your role or responsibility requires so much time that you've completely lost sight of what you wanted. Your partner, on the other hand, is full steam ahead on continuing the growth and piling on the plate to reach $1 million in revenue. This is a lose-lose situation for everyone. If you aren't happy, it will affect your performance and your commitment. Your partner will lose because they won't have your full drive.

Before partnering with someone, have this discussion about goals. This is almost as important as analyzing the deal you are about to invest in together. Here are some questions to ask your partner that you should also ask yourself:

- Why do you want to invest in this deal?

- Where do you see yourself in five years?
- What are some of your previous goals?
- Do you have a plan in place for your life?
- What is really important to you now?
- What would it take in order to view yourself as successful?

Making a Plan of Action Steps

Once you have your S.M.A.R.T. goal, how will you build action items that you take to achieve that goal?

There are steps you can take every day, every week, and every month that will make your goal a reality. Lay out what those steps are. They are often referred to as M.I.N.S.—the most important next step.

Just like you want your goal to be measurable, you'll want your action steps to be measurable as well. For example, "I will make fifteen cold calls a day to potential sellers." This is a better action step than something general, such as "I'll make cold calls to sellers every day."

BRAINSTORM

If this is your first deal ever, you may not know what those action steps are yet. As you go along, you'll have to pivot and change them. Even if you are experienced as an investor, you still may not know the exact steps to make your goal happen, and it can take some trial and error.

This is a practice you can do on your own, but if you really want to maximize that effort, take the opportunity to involve your partner. Create action steps together that align with your roles and the responsibilities of the company.

I like using whiteboards to lay out a good brainstorm. You also can use pen and paper, the Miro app, or large sticky notes. Even if something seems like a bad idea, throw it up there—it could lead to a good idea. Plus, the more information you write down, the more detailed your action items can be.

As you go through this exercise with your partner, think back to middle school or high school. What did you learn when working together as a team with other kids? In order to work well with others, you must listen and attempt to understand while avoiding criticism, jumping to conclusions, and shooting down poor ideas. You know all of this, but it's so easy to forget!

These types of brainstorming sessions can be energetic and fulfilling, or they can be a drag and seem like a waste of time. Before you even put together an agenda for how the brainstorm will go, set a time and location for it to take place. Don't just decide on a whim one day that you want to talk about goal setting and planning. Let each partner have time to adequately prepare.

Preparing for a Goal-Alignment Meeting

Before attending your goal-setting meeting, know what your goals are and any action items that you have off the top of your head. Once you're in the meeting, you may discover that your goals have shifted and that your partners have helped you define better, stronger action items. Still, you should at least go into the meeting with an idea of what you want to accomplish and how you want your life to be. Make a list of things that are important to you and to the business.

Part of your preparation could be a reading assignment. Some book recommendations: *Vivid Vision*, *Traction*, *Rocket Fuel*, and *Profit First*. *Vivid Vision* can help you with goal setting. *Traction* and *Rocket Fuel* can help with planning your business and creating an outline. *Profit First* is focused on systems and processes to maximize profit in your business.

MEETING LOCATION

Besides doing your homework, establish a time and place for the meeting. This could be a full day blocked out, a weekend retreat, or even just a quiet dinner. The setting is actually quite important. You don't want a ton of distractions, and you want to be able to communicate openly to each other. It should be a safe place to do that, as corny as it sounds. A rock concert may not be the best place to have a discussion. Our real estate investor friends Tyler and Zosia Madden book an annual family weekend in the mountains where they dream big and turn those dreams into goals. They take the weekend to relax, understand each other, and build out their business.

There is no wrong way to do it unless it's not working. This may mean quarantining in a conference room or renting a room at a restaurant while enjoying dinner and drinks. If you have an office or work out of your house, it can be beneficial to get away from any distractions that may pop up. Even consider the option of being unreachable that day. With cell phones powered off, you can be laser focused on the task at hand.

THE CRITICAL SKILL OF LISTENING

It's important to remember to use your basic communication skills—in *every* meeting.

There's a great book by Kate Murphy called *You're Not Listening,* and the lesson that I took away from it is that a lot of people are too busy thinking about their response before someone even finishes speaking. We've caught ourselves doing this plenty of times, and it has been something we've continually worked on. As podcast hosts, it's imperative to be good listeners. Yes, we have to ask great questions, but the real gold comes from our guests' answers.

We must be conscientious and actually listen so that we can ask better questions, rather than just focusing on what question we plan to ask next.

AGENDA

When you attend a networking event, you should have a clear intention of why you are going to the event and what you want out of it; the same goes for your alignment meeting. There is nothing worse than an unproductive meeting.

Here's a sample agenda you can use to start your alignment and get it into motion.

- Give each person an allotted amount of time to state their goals. These should be both personal and business goals. There shouldn't be any comments or criticism on the goals as each person goes around the room sharing.

- Next, make a list of the commonalities. Use that to start a brainstorm of things that are important to the partners and the business.
- Start forming items off the brainstorm into goals.
- After outlining some business goals, create a second brainstorm of action items. These are steps you can take to reach those goals. Assign each action item to a person whose role will be to stay on top of progressing that item. Don't get overeager with assigning roles and tasks. Let partners have the opportunity to volunteer to take on those items.
- If there is an action item that seems taxing and nobody wants to do it, then this is an opportunity to discuss outsourcing. Each of you most likely wanted to get into this business to get away from doing things you don't want to do. Use this time to figure out how you can outsource those burdens and keep filling your cup with action items that give you passion and life.

Everyone should walk away from the meeting with a clear plan of what they are responsible for and where the company is headed. It should be a clear route with checkpoints to make sure each person is in their lane and progressing.

TIMELINE

Every goal must have an ending. Parkinson's Law states that if you give yourself the proper amount of time to get something accomplished and no extra time, you will achieve it, but if you give yourself extra time, you will use that extra time to complete it. In short, the exact amount of time you give yourself is the exact amount of time it will take to complete your task.

An internal monologue may occur where you're telling yourself you're grinding and hustling because you've spent three hours to complete a task, when you really could have completed it in just two hours. This is something to be cautious of when setting a goal end date. When do you want to reach your goal, and what is an appropriate amount of time to reach that goal? *The 12-Week Year* by Brian Moran highlights how the intensity and urgency of a shorter window doesn't allow you to get complacent. If you are easily able to complete each action item and your goal seems too far, then move it up. Don't be afraid to push yourself.

Checkpoint Meetings

So, you have a plan in place to reach your business goals. Everyone is pumped up and ready to get to work and excited for the future! How long does that momentum actually last?

Have you ever attended a conference or networking event and left feeling so energized? Then when you get home real life hits, and all of a sudden the things you learned or wanted to implement are thrown out the window and put on the back burner?

Don't let this happen with your business. There are things you can do to keep the momentum going.

Set regular checkpoint or alignment meetings just to touch base and make sure everyone is on track. This could be a weekly or quarterly meeting. Keep a regular meeting on the calendar to discuss not only the day-to-day running of the business but also the long-term, strategic direction. This is great for holding each other accountable too. Each meeting can be brief because there is work to be done!

The meeting can consist of a review of the goals and the action items set, and then how everyone is successfully implementing those action items. This could be an opportunity to transition or pivot to make things more efficient. You may realize that a goal or an action item isn't even helping you progress toward your goal and is deemed a waste of time.

These meetings are also an opportunity to see if anything needs to be outsourced. Virtual assistants are a great resource and can be cost-effective. We have had success finding virtual assistants for small or recurring tasks from websites like Upwork and Fivver. It's not worth causing turmoil in your partnership by assigning a daunting task to your partner that can easily be assigned to someone else without breaking the bank.

The success of an alignment meeting is dependent on how truthful the partners are with each other. If there's an issue, it needs to be addressed head-on, and as quickly as possible. One of the fastest ways to wreck a partnership is to keep quiet on issues that are bothering you.

Goal Setting and Alignment Before Structure

Goal setting and alignment are important before getting a partner as well as during your partnership. Don't skimp on either one. In the next chapter, we are going to move into building the structure of your partnership, but we want you to keep this chapter in mind. It's easy to forget and get overzealous on the structure piece, but the structure piece won't work if you haven't implemented this chapter. Knowing each other's goals in addition to the goals of your business can actually help you determine what structure is right for you too. As you move forward, make sure these are completed first, *before* you begin building the components of the structure.

Chapter 6
PARTNERSHIP STRUCTURE

— Tony —

It's time to take everything you've learned so far in this book and put it to work as you start to craft the actual structure for your real estate partnership.

One of the questions we constantly get from our audience as hosts of the BiggerPockets *Real Estate Rookie* podcast is, How should I structure a partnership?

We've got good news and bad news for you.

The bad news is that we can't tell you what partnership structure makes sense for you. In fact, no book, podcast, or YouTube video can tell you what partnership structure makes sense for you. If you're looking for a magic one-size-fits-all answer that tells you exactly how to set up your partnership, then you need to reset your expectations.

The good news is that what we're going to give you is a framework you can use; once you understand this framework, you can apply it to your unique situation and craft a partnership structure that works for you and your partners. We will tell you all the different levers you can pull when structuring a partnership. Some of the levers may make sense for you to pull and others may make sense for you to ignore.

We'll cover the two types of real estate partnerships—debt partnerships and equity partnerships—and then we'll finish off with a few tips to help you structure your partnership in a way that reduces conflict and increases the chances of the partnership being successful long-term.

The goal is that by the end of this chapter, you'll have all the knowledge you need to create a partnership structure that is mutually beneficial for you and your partner.

Debt Partnerships

The first type of partnership we'll discuss is a debt partnership, or what's often referred to as a "private money" partnership.

In a debt partnership, Partner A lends money to Partner B, and in exchange, Partner B promises to repay Partner A with interest. We'll call the person who lends money the "lender" and the person who receives the money the "borrower." In this type of partnership, the borrower is the only person who owns the property. The lender has a lien against the property, which allows them to take over ownership only if the borrower defaults on the debt.

Debt partnerships are great if you're the lender because you can receive a relatively passive return on your cash that's both guaranteed *and* secured by a hard asset (the property). All you have to do as the lender is vet the borrower, wire your funds, and sign a few documents (which should be prepared and reviewed by an attorney).

Debt partnerships are great if you're the borrower because you get access to the capital that you need to close on a deal without giving up equity in that deal.

A debt partnership truly can be a win-win situation for both partners.

DEBT REPAYMENTS ARE GUARANTEED

While debt partnerships can be extremely powerful for the borrower, there are also some risks that are unique to these partnerships.

If you decide to enter into a debt partnership and you're the borrower, you're entering into an agreement to repay a debt. This is no different from getting a loan to purchase a car or getting a credit card. You're borrowing money from someone else, and the expectation is that you pay them back, with interest.

When you get a car loan, the bank doesn't care if you're short on cash because you had to buy new tires or replace your alternator. The bank wants their car payment from you on the first of the month, every single month.

The same is true of a debt partnership with real estate.

DOWNSIDE OF DEBT PARTNERSHIPS FOR THE BORROWER

In an equity partnership, which we'll cover in a bit, both partners participate in the upside *and* the downside of the property. For example, let's say your rental property experienced a big, unexpected expense this month. And say that the cash flow couldn't cover the expense *and* you didn't have enough money in your reserves to cover the cost. When this happens, it means your property is in the red, and you'll need to pay out of pocket to cover that expense.

Let's say you and your partner own a property together. That property produces $250 per month in cash flow. Let's also say that you have $1,500 in reserves for the property. Now imagine that you need to install a new electrical panel and the cost is $3,000. Between your cash flow ($250) and your reserves ($1,500), you have a total of $1,750 available to cover this cost, which means you're still short $1,250.

In an equity partnership, both partners would split the $1,250 evenly between the two of them, meaning each partner would contribute $625 toward the cost of the new panel.

But in a debt partnership, it's handled very differently.

Let's say you're the borrower and that you and the lender agreed that you would repay them $200 per month, every month, until the debt was repaid. In that scenario, even though the two of you technically "partnered" to purchase the property, you and you alone would be responsible for covering the entire $1,250 in addition to repaying your partner the $200 monthly payment that you owe them.

UPSIDE OF DEBT PARTNERSHIPS FOR THE BORROWER

Now, debt partnerships aren't all bad for the borrower. The benefits are substantial in this type of partnership when executed correctly.

In an equity partnership, you and the other partner are sharing ownership in the property. And when you share ownership, you also share in all the advantages that come along with owning the property, like appreciation, depreciation, rent increases, and other positives that come with owning the actual piece of real estate.

So, if you're in an equity partnership, and the value of the home increases by $100,000, you're splitting that $100,000 with your partner.

If you purchase a property and you're able to create a paper loss of $50,000 through depreciation and other write-offs, you're splitting that $50,000 with your partner.

If rents on the property increase from $1,000 in year one to $3,000 in year five, you're splitting that gain of $2,000 with your partner.

But in a debt partnership, none of those statements are true. In a debt partnership, the lender is not entitled to any of the property's appreciation, depreciation, income, or anything else; the lender is only entitled to the principal and interest payments. The only time the lender can tap into the value that comes from owning the property is if the borrower defaults and doesn't repay the money owed.

For the borrower, this means as long as you pay principal and interest payments on time and according to the agreement, you get to keep 100 percent of all the profits that come from owning the property.

THINGS TO INCLUDE IN A DEBT PARTNERSHIP

When entering into a debt partnership, whether you're the lender or the borrower, there are a few things you'll want to include:

- **Promissory Note**
  The promissory note is the agreement between the borrower and the lender, and it lays out all the details of the loan that's being issued.

- **Mortgage Security Document**

  The first document you'll need to secure your private money partnership is a mortgage security document. It takes different names depending on what state you're in (for example, it's called a "deed of trust" in California). The purpose of the mortgage security document is to tie the promissory note to the actual property. This document is typically notarized and submitted to the county that the property is located in.

  With the promissory note and the mortgage security document, in the unlikely event that the borrower defaults on the loan, the lender can then use these documents to foreclose on the property and try to recoup the money they lent. As the borrower or lender, you should have an understanding of the foreclosure process in your state.

- **Escrow Company**

  Whenever you're dealing with a loan that's connected to a piece of real estate, I'd recommend using an escrow company or a real estate attorney to handle all the funds. Depending on what state you close in, that state may require you to use a real estate attorney. (Note: As of press time, the following states require an attorney to close: Connecticut, Delaware, Georgia, Illinois, Massachusetts, New Jersey, New York, North Carolina, Vermont, and West Virginia.) This protects both the buyer and the seller. The escrow company works as an unbiased and unrelated third party that can make sure that the paperwork is correct and that the funds are used appropriately.

  We've probably all heard horror stories about relationships that go sour when one partner runs off with the money of another partner. Using an escrow company or real estate attorney can help reduce the chances of that happening.

When setting up a debt partnership, there are also a few items you need to clarify about the loan itself:

- **Interest Rate**

  First is your interest rate. Most lenders won't hand over their money out of the goodness of their hearts. Typically, they're going to want some type of return on their investment. And in a debt partnership, that "return" comes in the form of interest paid by the borrower.

You'll also want to clarify how that interest is calculated: Is it a simple interest rate? Or a more complicated calculation like APR?

In our business, we typically go with simple interest payments.

Now, determining what the interest should be is dependent upon a slew of factors:

What's the overall risk of the project? The riskier the project, the higher the interest rate will be. The less risky, the lower the interest rate will be. That's why U.S. Treasury bonds offer crazy low interest rates and why venture capitalists charge early-stage startups crazy-high interest rates. One of those is unremarkably safe, while the other is incredibly risky.

- **Term**
How long will the debt partnership last? Is it short-term (six to twelve months), medium term (two years to five years), or long-term (more than five years)? And what happens if you need to extend beyond the initial term?

The term that you and your partner agree on will be dependent on the type of project you're doing. If the project is a light, cosmetic rehab, then maybe a six-month term makes sense. If you're doing a full gut rehab where you're tearing a property down to the studs, then maybe eighteen months will make more sense. Think about how long it will take you to rehab the property and refinance the property to pay back your lender.

It's not a bad idea to add in a couple of months of buffer. For example, if you believe the rehab will take three months after closing and then two months to refinance with a bank, you would need five months, start to finish, for the project. If the rehab is delayed and takes longer than you estimated, or the bank can't get an appraiser out to your property in a timely manner, then any of these things could mess up your timeline. Set a month or two (or longer) as a buffer, especially if there is no prepayment penalty. If you end up finishing the property sooner than expected, you can pay off the debt partner with no consequences.

Some debt partners want a guarantee that they will get a certain amount of interest and will put into the contract that if the loan is repaid earlier than the term outlined in the contract, there is an additional fee; this could be a percentage of the loan balance. In the contract you can also outline terms if you do need an extension over the allotted amount of time.

Ashley recently did a private money loan where she opted to use her extension. This was a two-month extension where her interest rate went from 6.7 percent to 9 percent. For her, it was worth it to not rush through the project and to have it the way she wanted in order to maximize her appraisal and the cash-out refinance she was able to pull out of the property.

It's all about running the numbers and what will make sense for the deal. Work your contract around so that if you do need the extension, your numbers still work on the deal.

If the project is a commercial property, and the debt is being used to fund the initial purchase while one partner works on stabilizing and eventually refinancing into cheaper, long-term debt, then maybe the term needs to be three years.

In our business, we usually include an option to extend if the borrower needs more time, but the lender has the right to decline; if they approve, they'll usually receive an additional point or two in interest.

- **Payment Cadence**
When will payments on the loan be due? Will the lender require you to make payments monthly throughout the life of the loan? Quarterly? Or will there be no payments made during the life of the loan, and instead the borrower will just make one big payment at the end that includes all of the principal and interest payments?

As the borrower, it's obviously more advantageous to delay any payments until the project is complete. But as the lender, you may want to see some of your return come back immediately as opposed to waiting until the end of the term. However you set up the payments for your loan, you want to make sure it still works in your deal. If you can't afford to cover the monthly interest payments during the rehab of the property, you are going to be underwater before you even get started.

DEBT PARTNERSHIP EXAMPLE

Let's say that you enter into a debt partnership with the following details, and let's assume you're the borrower in this scenario.

- **Amount:** $250,000
- **Term:** Twelve months
- **Interest Rate:** 10 percent (simple interest)
- **Monthly Payments:** No

At the end of twelve months, you would've accrued $25,000 in interest (10 percent of $250,000). And let's say you use $200,000 to purchase the property and the remaining $50,000 goes toward renovations. When you close on the property, only your name will be on the deed. The loan from the lender will be listed as a lien against the property.

Since you made no monthly payments during the twelve-month term, you would only have one balloon payment due at the end of twelve months, for $275,000 ($25,000 in interest + $250,000 in principal).

Once you pay off your lender (and we'll assume that you refinanced with an actual bank), their lien is removed from the property, and now your new bank will have a lien against the property for the money they've lent to you.

TAX TREATMENT WITH DEBT PARTNERS
By Amanda Han, CPA

How you structure a deal can have significant impact when it comes to taxes. If you take on debt partners, the interest that you pay them is a tax deduction to you. This can help to reduce your taxable income. Additionally, because they are simply the lender and not an owner of the property, you get to keep all the tax benefits of that particular deal.

For example, if you were to borrow money to purchase a rental property, 100 percent of the tax deductions and depreciation belong to you as the property owner. The debt partner is a lender to this deal and is not entitled to any of those tax benefits because they have no ownership of the property.

Another benefit of taking on debt partners is that it can help keep your entity structures simpler. For example, you may have an LLC to hold three rental properties and have three different debt partners lending on the properties. This works just the same as if your LLC owned two rentals, and you obtained one loan from Bank of America and another loan from Wells Fargo. Alternatively, if you had three equity partners on three different properties, you would likely need to have separate LLCs to hold each of the properties. This can significantly increase your annual costs for legal and accounting fees and make it harder to scale as well.

Equity Partnerships

The second type of partnership we'll discuss is an equity partnership.

Unlike a debt partnership, where the borrower is the only person on the title and the only person who legally owns the property, an equity partnership means both people have ownership in the property. The actual percentage that each person owns will vary from one partnership to another.

Where debt partnerships are one-sided in the sense that only the borrower is responsible when a property's profits are down, in an equity partnership both partners share in the upside *and* the downside of a property.

And, just like debt partnerships, equity partnerships truly can be a win-win situation for both partners. Let's break down how we can structure an equity partnership by first looking at how each partner can contribute to this type of partnership.

THE TWO TYPES OF CONTRIBUTIONS

In an equity partnership, there are two key types of contributions that a partner can make: labor contributions and capital contributions.

A labor contribution is the actual work that goes into the real estate partnership.

With a capital contribution, each partner can either be a money partner or a non-money partner. A money partner is the person who brings the capital to cover the down payment, closing costs, reserves, rehab costs, and any other financial needs for the investment. A non-money partner is someone who doesn't bring any capital to the partnership but contributes in other meaningful ways.

LABOR CONTRIBUTIONS

Let's start our discussion by focusing on labor contributions.

Types of Labor Contribution

Oftentimes in a partnership, investors tend to overvalue the capital contribution and undervalue the labor contribution. But as important as the money is, if there's no one focused on using that money wisely, then good deals can quickly turn into bad deals.

There are different ways that someone can contribute to a partnership with their labor, so let's break a few of the big ones down.

- **Property Management**
  Once the property is purchased, someone has to take on the duty of managing the property on a day-to-day basis. And even if a third-party property manager is hired, someone still has to manage the property manager. This person is referred to as an "asset manager." When we mention property manager or asset manager, this encompasses short-term, mid-term, and long-term rental strategies.

Property management is hard. Just to give you a glimpse, Ashley spent her first several years as a property manager for eighty units in a windowless office with no AC, working late into the night, where she'd hide from the tenants and cry. She's come a long way since then, but still has the occasional cry.

Anyone who says property management isn't hard probably hasn't managed very many properties. There are ways to streamline, automate, and systemize, but any time you're dealing with people and their homes, there's potential for major headaches.

So the role of property manager is *crucial* in the partnership, and whoever steps into this role should have their contributions fairly valued.

Think for a moment about the differences in roles.

The money partner just has to sign a few docs and wire funds on closing day. The totality of their work is a few hours, at most.

But the non-money partner who takes on the role of property management is doing that job every single day, for as long as the partnership owns the property—that's a massive difference in time. And at some point—maybe it's one year in, maybe it's five years in—the value of that time eclipses the value of the money that was invested.

We'll talk a bit more about how to make sure the property manager in the partnership is fairly compensated, but for now, just understand that this is a very important role that impacts the majority of real estate partnerships.

- **Rehab**
Rehabbing properties is one of the best ways to maximize your returns as a real estate investor. Rehabbing entails buying a property that's in bad shape for a discounted price, then going through the painstaking work of taking it from a class D property to a class A property. As a reward for your hard work, the value of the property should increase to an amount that's higher than what you paid for it.

Sounds amazing, right?

Fortunes have been built rehabbing real estate investments. When it comes to your partnership, managing the rehab is a tremendous way to provide value. And luckily, there are a few different ways you can play a role in the rehab.

■ Self-Performer
If you're a handy person who knows their way around a toolbox, then maybe executing the labor needed to complete the rehab is the right role for you. Rehabs are one of the biggest struggles for new investors (oftentimes, experienced investors too), and if you are able to take that off their plate, that can be a huge value play.

■ General Contractor
If you're knowledgeable in the world of construction, but don't really like the idea of swinging hammers, then hiring and managing the subcontractors is a great way to provide value.

■ Project Manager
As the project manager, your main focus is managing the general contractor. And I mean no disrespect when I say this, but almost every general contractor I've met has needed *some* level of oversight to finish a job on budget and on time. Even if you don't necessarily have a ton of construction experience, if you're good at managing deadlines and people, then this could be a great role for you.

■ Bookkeeping and Accounting
Don't let your eyes glaze over just yet. Doing the bookkeeping and accounting for your real estate business is one of the most efficient ways to maintain profitability and reduce your tax liability.

Most investors who don't come from an accounting background don't pay much attention to their bookkeeping until it's too late. They find themselves scrambling as tax time comes around, and it becomes a hectic and stressful game of trying to figure out why they spent $23.49 on Amazon seven months ago.

If you naturally gravitate toward this part of the business, both you and your partners will be grateful come tax time.

- **Deal Finding**
  All the money in the world is pointless if you have no deals to invest in. Deal finding is a skill that some investors have developed better than others. If you have a penchant for scouring the MLS, cold-calling, door knocking, following up, and using your interpersonal skills to build relationships, then you can definitely add value to the partnership by being in charge of finding deals.
- **Deal Analysis**
  Once the hard work of finding deals is done, someone has to do the work of determining whether or not any of those deals in the pipeline have the potential to be profitable. If you're big on crunching numbers, finding comps, using the BiggerPockets calculators, and so on, then this is the seat for you.

Paying Hourly and Fixed Rates for Labor

A great way to ensure there's fairness in a partnership when it comes to labor is to assign an hourly rate or a fixed rate to all of the tasks being performed by the partners.

The actual dollar amount of the rate is totally up to you and your partner. It could be in line with what the market rate is for a similar task, or you could opt to do it on the cheap to save the partnership money. Ultimately, it's whatever you and your partner both feel is fair and reasonable.

One thing to be cautious of when you are implementing this pricing is that you are still running your numbers on the deal if you are outsourcing. You don't want to be paying your partner 5 percent to manage the property, and then one day your partner doesn't want to manage anymore, and it's 12 percent to hire a property management company. This ends up killing the cash flow on your property because you only projected a 5 percent management fee when determining your purchase price when buying the property.

What's more important is the timing. Ideally, you and your partner should decide on these rates up front. It becomes a *much* more awkward conversation when you're six months into a partnership and one of you has to say, *I don't like how we've set things up.*

For example, I handle the day-to-day management for all of our properties. And in some of my partnerships, in addition to the profit distribution I get as an owner, I also charge a management fee to the property that's in line with what other property managers would charge. I'm compensated both as an equity owner of the property and a service provider of the property. My partner and I consented to that agreement before we even closed on the property.

If you're the partner who's self-performing all of the rehab, then discuss with your partner what rate you feel is reasonable for the work you're doing. It could be a fixed rate for completing the demo, or it could be an hourly rate for all of the little miscellaneous tasks.

Ashley has an example similar to mine, where she received a property management fee for any long-term rental she owned with a specific partner. And while Ashley took care of the property management, her partner received an hourly rate for any maintenance and repair work he completed on the properties.

I've seen some partnerships where each person keeps a timesheet for all of the work they complete.

Again, the point here is that we want to make sure we're keeping a balance between the capital contributions and the labor contributions, Assigning "rates" for the labor helps make sure one partner doesn't feel taken advantage of. There is nothing that can ruin a relationship faster than the feeling of something being unfair. Paying rates for labor contributions helps mitigate that.

Profit Distributions vs. Salaries

When you and a partner own a real estate business together, there are two ways you can pay yourselves: an Owner's Pay account and a profit account. This idea has been popularized in many books, but my favorite explanation comes from the book *Profit First* by Mike Michalowicz. The author urges entrepreneurs to pay themselves using two separate checking accounts.

The first checking account is called your "owner's pay" account and is used to compensate you for the work that you do in the business. We just listed all of the ways you can contribute to your partnership with your labor—those are the activities that you would pay yourself for out of this account.

Payments are made from your owner's pay account on a frequent basis, in the same way you would pay an employee (think weekly, biweekly, or monthly).

Be sure to speak with a CPA about the correct way to pay yourself as there are limitations based on the entity structure of your company. For example, oftentimes as a member of an LLC, you cannot put yourself on payroll and receive a W-2 at the end of the year.

The second account is called your "profit" account, and it's used to compensate you for owning the business. When you pay yourself out of this account, you're not being paid for any of the work you're doing on a daily basis. Instead, you're paying yourself simply because you own the real estate business.

Payments from your profit account are made less frequently (think quarterly).

What's cool about this two-account method for paying yourselves is that it gives you another way of splitting the cash flow and can also help ensure fairness in how each partner is compensated in the business. For example, if Partner A is doing the majority of the work, they'll be compensated out of both the owner's pay biweekly and the profit account every quarter. And if Partner B is more of a silent partner, maybe they're only compensated out of the profit account once a quarter.

CAPITAL CONTRIBUTIONS

Now that we've covered labor contributions, let's look at the other type: capital contributions.

Types of Capital Contribution

Just as there are different ways to contribute with your labor, there are different ways you can contribute with your capital. It's also important for your partnership to clearly state exactly how that money partner is going to be paid back. We'll go through these options in a bit more detail.

- **Down Payment and Closing Costs**

  The most common way that money partners contribute to a partnership is by covering the costs associated with buying the property. This is typically your down payment and any closing costs.

  This cost can be carried completely by one partner, equally by both partners, or a different percentage split between the partners. In our business, we've used all three of those options.

  In some partnerships, our partners brought 100 percent of the capital that was needed. In other partnerships, we split it down the middle, with each of us bringing 50 percent of the capital. And in other situations, it was some other split, like a 75/25 or a 60/40. The partnership structure varied based on how much capital we had available, how many deals we needed to close at one time, and what type of structure ultimately made everyone happy.

- **Shortfalls**

  A shortfall is what happens when your property isn't profitable. It could be that there was an unexpected expense that wiped out all of your reserves, or maybe the property sat vacant for longer than you anticipated. Either way, the money the property generated wasn't enough to cover the expenses of owning that property.

  You and your partner have to think through what happens in that situation. If one partner brought all of the initial capital, is that same partner responsible in this situation? Or does the non-money partner need to cover the bill since they didn't help financially to begin with? Or do you go with the simple solution of splitting it down the middle?

  Again, the decision you make isn't important; what's important is that you talk about this beforehand, and get aligned on how you'll handle it.

SHORTFALL EXAMPLE
The Shreveport House

We had a major shortfall in one of my business partnerships. We owned a house in Shreveport, Louisiana, that was profitable over the first year that we owned it. But once the tenant's lease was up, we decided to exit that market and sell the property.

Unfortunately, the tenant didn't take the best care of the property, so immediately after the tenant left, we had to make some minor repairs before listing the property. Once the property was finally listed, we had to drop the price several times.

Eventually, we found a buyer, and as that buyer was going through their due diligence, they completed a property inspection. That inspection revealed a small leak under the floor in the living room that caused some pretty significant damage to the subfloor. Needless to say, that buyer backed out, and we had to invest a significant amount of money to replace the floor.

The property sat on the market for a few months (properties that get relisted have a stigma), but after a few more price drops, we eventually sold the property.

But instead of getting a big check at closing, we had to *write* a check because we sold for slightly less than our loan balance. All told, between the mortgage payments, the repair costs, and the closing costs, we lost about $30,000 on this property.

Why is this relevant? Because in our partnership, we made the agreement that any shortfall would be split evenly between us. My partner paid $15,000 and I paid $15,000.

Capital Recapture

So we know how the capital is being used, but how does the money partner get paid back? That's where the capital recapture comes into play.

When we use the phrase "capital recapture" in real estate investing, what we're asking ourselves is, Should the money partner get paid back as a priority before the non-money partner?

If you say yes to including a capital recapture in your real estate partnership, it basically means that before any of the profits are split between the partners, a portion (or all) of the profits is used to pay back the money partner.

Let's look at a few ways you can set up a capital recapture in your partnership.

- **Recapture through Cash Flow**

  If the capital recapture is handled through the cash flow, it means that a certain percentage of the profits is used to pay back the money partner. It could mean that 100 percent of the profits go back to the money partner until they're repaid. Or it could mean that 10 percent of the profits go back to the money partner, then the remaining 90 percent is split between the money partner and the non-money partner.

- **Recapture through a Fixed Amount**

  Another option to use the capital recapture is with a fixed amount. This means that every month (or whatever time frame the partners choose), a specific dollar amount is set aside from the profits to repay the money partner. If there are no profits, the money partner doesn't get repaid. Or if there are profits, but not enough to fully repay the fixed amount, then 100 percent of the profits would go to the money partner, and the balance would roll into the following month.

- **Recapture at Sale**

  If the capital recapture is handled through the sale of the property, it means that before any profits are split between the money partner and the non-money partner, the money partner is first repaid their initial investment, and then what's left over is split between the two partners.

◼ Examples of Each Type of Capital Recapture

Let's go through examples of how the capital recapture would work with these different scenarios.

Here are the details of our example property:

- **Cash Investment from Money Partner:** $100,000
- **Monthly Cash Flow:** $1,000

- **Proceeds from Sale:** $225,000
- **Money Partner Equity:** 50 percent
- **Non-Money Partner Equity:** 50 percent

■ Recapture through Cash Flow

Say that the two partners agree to allocate 100 percent of the monthly cash flow toward repaying the money partner. This means that each month, the money partner would receive $1,000 per month, and the non-money partner would receive $0. This would go on for eight years and four months. After that, the money partner would have received one hundred payments of $1,000 (equaling $100,000), and their initial cash investment is now "recaptured." From then on, the two partners would split the $1,000 per month, with each receiving $500 per month in cash flow.

In another scenario, the partners could agree to say that the money partner receives 60 percent of the cash flow as a capital recapture, and the remaining 40 percent is split 50/50. In this scenario, the money partner would receive $600 every month (60 percent of $1,000), leaving $400 per month for the two partners to split. This would go on for a total of 167 months (or about fourteen years).

If there was ever a month where the property didn't turn a profit, then the money partner simply wouldn't get their $600, and another month would be added to the repayment schedule (taking it from 167 months to 168 months).

And if there was a month where profits were $800 instead of $1,000, then the money partner would receive $480 (60 percent of $800) and the remaining $320 would be split 50/50, with each partner receiving $160.

■ Recapture through a Fixed Amount

This process is similar to recapture through cash flow, but the key difference here is that the repayment amount is not based on the cash flow. Whether the cash flow is $600, $1,000, or $2,000, the amount paid to the money partner remains the same.

Say that the two partners agree that the money partner is to be repaid $500 per month. It means the money partner gets the $500 every single month, regardless of what the profits are for that month.

■ Recapture at Sale

The profits from the sale of this property are $225,000, but the money partner invested $100,000. This means that before the two partners split the profits 50/50, the money partner is repaid their initial $100,000 investment, and then the remaining $125,000 is split 50/50.

So the money partner receives a total of $162,500 (their initial $100,000 investment plus 50 percent of $125,000) and the non-money partner receives $62,500.

WHAT ABOUT THE MORTGAGE?

In addition to labor and capital, a third piece of the puzzle is the mortgage. Unless you're buying your property with cash, you'll have to get a loan from a bank. And there are different ways you can structure the mortgage with your partnership.

- **One Person**

  If you opt for personal debt over commercial debt, then you could set it up so that only one person carries the mortgage. Obviously, this puts more risk on the partner who's carrying the mortgage. But if all they're doing is signing the loan docs, and the other partner is doing everything else, then the return might be worth the risk.

  There might be some situations where having just one person on the mortgage makes the most sense. If one partner is able to get approved for the loan on their own, then the partnership benefits because it then frees up the other partner's debt-to-income ratio to get approved for the next loan.

  But if both partners are applying for every loan together, even though they'd get approved individually, then they're limiting the number of loans they can get approved for.

- **Multiple People**

  In some situations, both partners have to be on the loan to get approved. This is what led to my first partnership. I had a great property under contract, but the bank said my debt-to-income ratio would be too high with that new mortgage, so I brought in a partner who was able to add his balance sheet to the loan and clear the path toward purchasing the property.

- **Limited Liability Company (LLC)**

  If you go the commercial route, then you and your partner can set up a new LLC where you're both owners, and then apply for the mortgage with that new LLC. A commercial lender will give you better terms if you sign as a personal guarantor on the loan. This means the LLC is not just liable, but you are also a member of the LLC.

  Most banks will require anyone with more than 20 percent ownership in the LLC to sign as a personal guarantor. This is something to consider when creating your structure if you are going to get a commercial loan. If there is someone who doesn't want to be a personal guarantor, one way to guarantee the bank won't require them is if they have less than 20 percent ownership.

  As you should with any lender, not only commercial, ask about their loan requirements *before* you structure any partnership that is going to rely on bank financing, and especially if there are some technicalities as to who can be on the loan. The lender is one person whom people usually forget to consult in their entity structure.

EQUITY PARTNERSHIP EXAMPLE

I want to make it abundantly clear that there is no right or wrong way to structure your partnership. However, I want to provide an actual example of how we structured one of our equity partnerships.

Responsibilities
- **Property Management:** Me
- **Rehab:** N/A

- **Bookkeeping:** Me
- **Deal Finding:** Me
- **Deal Analysis:** Me
- **Down Payment and Closing Costs:** 75 percent Partner / 25 percent Me
- **Mortgage:** Partner

Equity
- **Equity:** 75 percent Partner / 25 percent Me
- **Profits:** 75 percent Partner / 25 percent Me
- **Property Management Fee:** 15 percent to Me

Essentially, my team and I did all the work of finding the deal, setting the property up, and managing it day-to-day. My partner carried the mortgage and brought 75 percent of the capital. I brought the other 25 percent of the capital required. This consisted of the down payment, start-up costs, furnishings, and closing costs. We agreed to split equity and profits so that it matched our capital contributions. In addition, we agreed to take a 15 percent management fee to account for all of the work we did daily.

TAX TREATMENT WITH EQUITY PARTNERS
By Amanda Han, CPA

Tenants-in-Common

When you take on equity partners, this means that you jointly own the real estate. Regardless of whether you hold title as tenants-in-common or in a legal entity such as an LLC, the income, expenses, and tax benefits are shared between you and the partner(s).

What a lot of people don't know is that when you own properties as tenants-in-common, all the income and expenses should be split based on ownership percentage. If you own 60 percent of the property and your partner owns 40 percent, 60 percent of the income should go to you, and 60 percent of expenses should be paid by you. Similarly, 40 percent of the income should go to your partner, and 40 percent of the expenses should be paid by your partner.

Purely from a tax perspective, tenant-in-common ownership provides simplicity when it comes to tax filings. There is no separate tax return to be filed if you are each only holding title in your personal names. In our example, you simply report 60 percent of the income and expenses of the property on your personal taxes, and your partner will report their share on their own taxes.

An added benefit of this structure is that you are separate owners and thus can make separate decisions. This becomes important if you do not agree on what you want to do when it is time to sell the property. For example, you may decide that you want to use a 1031 exchange to defer the capital gains taxes you might owe when this property sells. However, your partner may not want to do this because maybe they have losses that they can use to offset the gain or they want to use the cash for other non–real estate things. Because this is structured as a tenants-in-common ownership, you are free to 1031 exchange your portion of the transaction. This has no impact on what your partner decides (and vice versa). They can choose to pay the tax, and it does not limit your 1031 exchange at all.

Similarly, during the years when you're holding onto the rental property, you may decide you want to take accelerated depreciation and use that to offset taxes from your other income. But for other personal reasons, your partner may not find this to be beneficial. As tenants-in-common owners, each of you can decide which of these strategies you want to use without impacting the other party.

Although the tenant-in-common structure might seem like a good idea, there are certainly some significant legal concerns and pitfalls to watch out for, so be sure to check with your attorney before moving forward.

LLC Partnership

The most frequent structure that we see when it comes to partnering is to hold title in an LLC. In this scenario, a new LLC is formed for this deal. Typically, you and your partner will be members of this LLC. From a tax perspective, the LLC is usually treated as a partnership. This means that the LLC will file a separate federal and state partnership tax return. The rental income and expenses are first reported on the LLC's partnership tax return. Generally, these entities are considered flow-through entities. In the tax world, it simply means that the entity is not paying any income taxes. Rather, the taxable income or loss will flow through to the members' personal tax returns.

Although a little more complex when it comes to tax filing, one of the benefits of LLC partnership is that it helps to combine the reporting requirements into one entity. This is especially helpful if your partner is not well versed in the financial and tax aspects of investing and does not want the hassle of having to report the details of these on their tax returns. Once your accountant prepares the LLC partnership's tax return, a Schedule K-1 will be generated to show your and your partner's share of the net income or loss. Simply send that K-1 to your partner, and they can easily add that number to their own tax returns.

Besides the streamlined reporting on the tax side, there are typically asset protection benefits to owning a rental in an LLC rather than just in your personal name. But one of the downsides of this LLC structure is the annual cost of having to maintain and file tax returns each year. As you scale and have a lot of different partners in different deals, these costs can add up quickly.

Another tax downside of using an LLC partnership structure is that there is less flexibility when it comes to tax planning. Decisions on how to report certain items and what strategies are used need to be made at the partnership level.

For example, if you wanted to do a cost segregation study to increase your depreciation this year, but your partner does not want to do that, this would be an issue. Before the tax return is filed, you both need to come to an agreement on whether or not the LLC will do a cost segregation study. Similarly, when it's time to sell the property, you must jointly agree on whether or not the LLC will do a 1031 exchange to defer the capital gains taxes. And if it was decided that a 1031 exchange was to be done, the new replacement property must also be purchased inside this jointly owned LLC.

Because the properties are owned in the LLC, these types of decisions can no longer just be made by the partners individually. As with most other things in partnering, it is important to make sure you get clarity on these important decisions prior to entering into that business relationship.

Other Structures

There is another common method of entity structuring that involves both tenant-in-common and LLCs. In this example, the rental property is held as tenant-in-common, just like I explained above. But instead of you and your partner personally owning that tenant-in-common interest, it could be owned by each of your own LLCs.

This could be a scenario where the property on Main Street is held as tenant-in-common by two parties: One party is John Smith, LLC, and the other is Jane Doe, LLC. This type of structure can help to give some level of liability protection and also provide flexibility when it comes to taxes.

One important thing to keep in mind is that when it comes to partnering, tax planning, and asset protection, there is no one-size-fits-all. Make sure to do proper planning with your team of advisors before entering into these business arrangements.

Starting Small with Your Partnership

Starting small can take different shapes, but ideally, you can start small using one of these two options.

LOW COST

Can you enter into the partnership with a nominal amount of money invested? The amount will vary from person to person, and it requires you to look at your own financial situation. But ultimately, you can consider it low-cost if you can stomach losing the money you're investing into the partnership.

What you should absolutely avoid is investing your entire life savings or your very last penny into a deal with someone you barely know or you've never worked with before.

SHORT TERM

Can you set the partnership up so that it's relatively short-term? An example would be focusing on transactional partnerships *before* holding any real estate together long-term.

Transactional deals in real estate investing are activities like flipping and wholesaling. These are deals that can be completed within a few months and don't require any long-term commitments to each other. Once a house flip is complete, you and the other person can decide to do another one or never work with each other again. The benefit is that you're not locked into a property in the same way you would be if you owned a rental together.

Putting Your Partnership Structure in Writing

The brain is a remarkable thing. There are billions of neurons in our brains, and they move information at lightning-fast speeds. The brain controls our ability to speak, walk, run, dance, and sing. It controls our ability to do complex math equations or write books on real estate partnerships. The brain also stores all of our memories.

But one shortcoming of the brain? It doesn't remember things perfectly. In fact, research has shown that our memories are malleable, meaning that how we remember things changes over time. And each time our brain "retrieves" a memory, that memory can get shifted and rewritten to include new details that didn't really happen or exclude details that *did* happen.

So how does this affect your business partnership? The short story is, if the details of your business partnership aren't memorialized in some way, then chances are either you or your partner (or both of you) will forget the details of how you structured that partnership.

Every partnership we've entered into has had some form of written document that outlines everything we agreed on regarding the partnership.

This is such an effective way to manage your partnership because any time there's a question on what to do in a certain situation, or what we said we were going to do, instead of debating and bickering, you can go back to the written structure.

When you create that written document, it should include everything we've covered in this chapter so far, plus more, as we continue through this book. What are the different ways each partner will contribute with their labor? Will you compensate each partner based on an hourly rate for the work they'll be doing? Will you provide profit distributions and, if so, with what frequency? How will each partner be paid back for the capital they contributed to the partnership? What happens if the partnership runs out of money?

As you work through all of these answers, put them in writing and use that as the foundation for your partnership agreement. Speaking of, the partnership agreement (also called an operating agreement) is an important document that outlines the terms of the partnership. Here's an example:

OPERATING AGREEMENT OF [LLC NAME]

This Operating Agreement (the "Agreement") is made and entered into as of the [Date] by and between PARTNER 1 and PARTNER 2 (collectively, the "Members"), for the purpose of forming a limited liability company (the "Company") under the laws of the State of New York.

ARTICLE I. FORMATION

1.1 Formation. The Members hereby form a limited liability company under the name of [LLC Name] (the "Company") in accordance with the laws of the State of New York.

1.2 Purpose. The purpose of the Company is to purchase and manage a rental property located at [Address] (the "Property").

ARTICLE II. CAPITAL CONTRIBUTIONS

2.1 Initial Contributions. The initial capital contribution of each Member shall be as follows:

-
-

2.2 Additional Contributions. If additional capital contributions are required for the operation of the Company or the maintenance of the Property, each Member shall contribute such additional funds in proportion to their respective ownership interests in the Company.

2.3 Loans. The Members may agree to lend funds to the Company for the operation of the Company or the maintenance of the Property. Any loans made by a Member shall be considered an additional capital contribution and shall be repaid in accordance with the terms of the loan agreement.

ARTICLE III. MANAGEMENT

3.1 Management. The Members shall manage the Company in accordance with the terms of this Agreement.

3.2 Meetings. The Members shall meet at least annually to review the Company's financial statements, discuss the Property's performance, and make any necessary decisions regarding the operation of the Company.

3.3 Decision-Making. Decisions regarding the operation of the Company shall be made by unanimous vote of the Members.

ARTICLE IV. ALLOCATION OF PROFITS AND LOSSES

4.1 Allocation. Profits and losses of the Company shall be allocated to the Members in proportion to their respective ownership interests in the Company.

ARTICLE V. DISTRIBUTIONS

5.1 Distributions. Distributions shall be made to the Members in proportion to their respective ownership interests in the Company, as determined by the Members.

ARTICLE VI. TRANSFER OF INTERESTS

6.1 Transfer. A Member may not transfer or assign their interest in the Company without the prior written consent of the other Member.

ARTICLE VII. DISSOLUTION

7.1 Dissolution. The Company shall be dissolved upon the unanimous decision of the Members or as required by law.

7.2 Liquidation. Upon the dissolution of the Company, the Property shall be sold and the proceeds distributed to the Members in proportion to their respective ownership interests in the Company.

ARTICLE VIII. GENERAL PROVISIONS

8.1 Governing Law. This Agreement shall be governed by and construed in accordance with the laws of the State of New York.

8.2 Entire Agreement. This Agreement contains the entire understanding of the Members with respect to the Company and supersedes all prior negotiations, understandings, and agreements between the Members.

8.3 Amendments. This Agreement may be amended or modified only by the unanimous written consent of the Members.

IN WITNESS WHEREOF, the Members have executed this Agreement as of the date first written above.

Partner 1 Name

Partner 2 Name

LLC vs. Joint Venture Agreements

Now that you understand the importance of putting your partnership structure in writing, let's explore how you can formally create that structure.

The two options most prevalent in my real estate business are creating a new limited liability company (LLC) or creating a joint venture (JV) agreement between two existing entities. Those will be the options we'll discuss here.

As a caveat, we (Ashley and Tony) are not attorneys, and we are not CPAs. The information we're going to provide here and throughout this book is meant only to serve as a starting point for your conversation with a true professional on this topic.

WHAT'S THE DIFFERENCE BETWEEN AN LLC AND A JOINT VENTURE?

Let's talk through some of the key differences between an LLC and a JV agreement.

With an LLC, you and your partner create an entirely new business entity together. With a JV agreement, you're creating an agreement on how two separate entities will work together. The difference might be best described through an example.

Let's say John and Jane want to purchase a real estate investment together, and they decide to create a new LLC named J&J LLC. John and Jane are both listed as owners of J&J LLC. They draft an operating agreement and state that they each own 50 percent of the LLC. They go out and purchase their real estate investment and J&J LLC is listed on the deed of the property, as well as the mortgage. All of the income and expenses flow from a bank account owned by J&J LLC. And every month, John and Jane each take a profit distribution from that bank account. At the end of the year, John and Jane hire a CPA to file a tax return for J&J LLC.

In another scenario, let's say John and Jane decide to create a JV agreement. John has his own LLC (John's LLC), and Jane has her own LLC (Jane's LLC), and those two LLCs enter into a contract with one another. John's LLC and Jane's LLC both remain totally separate, but they agree to share in the management and ownership of the new property. They draft a JV agreement that clearly states what each LLC will contribute to the joint venture, how the profits and losses will be shared, the length of the partnership, and so on.

They go out and purchase their real estate investment, and on the deed John's LLC is listed as 50 percent owner and Jane's LLC is listed as 50 percent owner. All of the income and expenses flow through a bank account that is jointly owned by both LLCs. They still make profit distributions monthly. And at the end of the year, John's LLC recognizes 50 percent of the profits from the partnership, and Jane's LLC recognizes the other 50 percent of the profits.

Revisiting Your Partnership Structure

Here's the thing: When you enter into a real estate partnership, both you and your partner are making many assumptions about how that partnership will operate.

You'll make assumptions about:

- How you'll balance the workload.
- How much time each of you will be able to dedicate to the partnership on a regular basis.
- The impact that each of your roles will have on the partnership.
- Which roles each of you will enjoy and will want to continue to perform.

But sometimes (and this is especially true if both of you are new to real estate) those assumptions are going to be completely wrong.

For example, maybe you assign yourself to focus on acquisitions while your partner focuses on operations. And since it's an even split in responsibilities, you decide to split the profits and equity right down the middle, 50/50.

But after a year of working together, the reality is that your partner turned out to be even better than you at acquisitions. They found six of the ten deals that your partnership purchased, *and* they still managed all of the acquisitions. Does 50/50 still make sense?

Or maybe you were supposed to be the money partner who provided the down payment and carried the mortgage, and your partner was supposed to take care of everything else. And say the two of you agree to a 60/40 split (60 to you), plus a 15 percent management fee to your partner for doing the day-to-day management.

But six months down the road, you realize that you've taken more calls from tenants than your partner has, *and* you ended up being the one managing the books. Does it still make sense for 15 percent to go to your partner?

So what's the solution?

GET CLEAR UP FRONT

First, both you and your partner should enter into the partnership with a clear understanding that the current partnership structure is based on assumptions and is not set in stone. Having that clarity at the beginning will make it so much easier to adjust the structure when the time comes.

IT'S OKAY TO MAKE CHANGES TO AN AGREEMENT

In the United States, the Constitution was officially ratified on June 21, 1788. This important document became the framework of the government. Countless hours and brainpower were poured into creating it.

But do you know what happened just three and a half years later, on December 15, 1791? The government assembled and made not one but *ten* changes to the Constitution! These changes, or amendments, became known as the Bill of Rights.

Essentially, the government came together and said, We need to make a few changes to get this thing right.

Since then, there have been a total of twenty-seven amendments to the Constitution.

Why, in a book about real estate partnerships, are we taking a detour to your fifth-grade history class? Well, if an organization as big and complex as the United States government can make changes to how it runs an entire country, then surely you and your business partner should get together every so often and make changes to how you structure your real estate partnership.

REVIEW YOUR STRUCTURE REGULARLY

At some regular cadence, you and your partner should be revisiting the structure of your partnership to make sure it's still fair and that no partner feels that either side is being taken advantage of. Set timelines in your agreement that state when those meetings should take place.

It's great to have this as a talking point during your quarterly or annual meetings.

These conversations have the potential to get awkward—fast—but push through the awkwardness because the partnership will be much better off with both of you being honest and transparent about how you feel.

In fact, almost nothing can kill a partnership faster than not being open and communicative. If one partner is feeling slighted but doesn't have the courage to speak up, that feeling can quickly grow into resentment. And resentment in a partnership is hard to overcome.

To prevent that from happening, always include a structure review as part of your regular partnership meetings.

The Bottom Line

Hopefully after reading through this chapter you have a strong understanding of the different elements you should consider when creating the structure for your real estate partnership. Remember, there is no one-size-fits-all solution.

And at the end of the day, the only thing that *really* matters is that you and your potential partner feel that the structure is fair and reasonable, along with a layer of protection for both of you.

Chapter 7
MEMOIRS OF PARTNERSHIP

— *Tony and Ashley* —

By this point, you've learned there are many variables that go into building a partnership: the structure of it, the equity, the responsibilities, the capital, the profit share.

We know it would be great to have someone tell you outright how to structure a real estate partnership—but since each partnership has different needs, we can't tell you exactly how you should structure yours. Instead, we're going to walk you through some examples of *our* partnerships so you can see how we structured them, what worked, and even what didn't work. Take what you can from each example and tailor it to fit what's right for you and your partner.

Ashley's Partnership Example 1
WHY I NEEDED A PARTNER

At the beginning of my investment career, I worked for an investor who would do a cash-out refinance on a property, then use that cash to purchase another property. I wanted to buy real estate, but I had this limited mindset that you had to pay for an investment property in cash, which I didn't have enough of. Instead of finding different ways to fund deals on my own, I searched for a partner who had the money.

HOW I FOUND A PARTNER

I had a childhood friend who had an interest in investing like his father did. He didn't have any current investment properties, besides his primary residence, and had done a great job of saving money. We discussed options, strategies, and what we could each bring to the table. At this point I was working as a property manager and understood the market and long-term rentals. I was confident I could find a deal. That deal happened to be the first duplex we looked at. I analyzed the deal and presented it to my friend. It was very nerve-racking for both of us. I distinctly remember him looking at me and saying, "I'm putting a lot of trust into you."

This partner (we'll call him Scott) was going to fund the deal with his life savings of $70,000, a large amount of money for both of us. The idea was to do the BRRRR strategy, though we didn't know that term at the time. We would fix up both units of the duplex, rent them out, and then refinance to buy another property. We didn't do it exactly that way, but that was the idea.

We walked the property together, and Scott ended up bringing even more value by asking his roommate (Scott was house hacking, though we didn't know that term yet either) to do some of the labor for the rehab in exchange for a decrease in his monthly rent. That definitely helped our bottom line. The major expenses for the rehab would be new vinyl plank flooring, paint, a heat and AC split unit, kitchen cabinets in one unit, and a new electrical panel. We had a piece of paper with our rehab estimates on it. Let me tell you, it was rough. There wasn't a lot of detail, and it was our best guess. I used my savings to fund the rehab costs.

After we had the property under contract, we went to work on the structure of the LLC we would be forming. This is something important to note: *If you don't already have an LLC formed, you don't have to form one until you get the property under contract.* Don't pay fees to maintain an LLC until you actually have a property. When you get a property under contract but don't have the LLC formed yet, you can have the contract state your name or another entity with "and/or assigns as," commonly seen as AOAA. This way you can change the name on the contract to the new LLC you have formed.

We also had agreed upon a partnership structure *before* buying the property. Ours was a verbal agreement, but I strongly recommend putting it in writing to prevent any memory loss from either party.

HOW WE STRUCTURED THE PARTNERSHIP

We decided we would be 50/50 partners in the LLC. Each of us would have 50 percent equity and receive 50 percent of the cash flow. Scott was supplying the cash to purchase the first property. We set it up as if he were the bank holding the mortgage. We amortized the $70,000 over fifteen years at 5.5 percent. He would receive monthly payments, just as if we were paying the bank. We drew up a loan agreement with the repayment terms. Scott was getting his principal paid back and making 5.5 percent in interest on the money he loaned our LLC, along with 50 percent of the cash flow each month.

For each property going forward, we continued this setup but started using OPM (other people's money) or seller financing until we eventually didn't need Scott to put in any more capital.

Part of our structure was that I do all the legwork: find the deal, run the numbers, handle the closing, do the leasing, and manage the property. Scott provided the money and was the silent partner. That's what we agreed on.

It wasn't unfair; we both were happy with that arrangement. It was a great deal for Scott. I was ecstatic that someone was going to trust me with that large amount of money and get me into my first deal. I wouldn't do that structure today because I now put a high value on doing the legwork. Still, looking back on it, I wouldn't change it because it got me started and propelled my addiction to real estate deals.

We have now done six real estate deals together, maintaining our LLC with 50/50 partnership. On other deals, Scott has also been a private money lender for me where he doesn't have any equity but provides a short-term loan at 10 percent interest.

Tony's Partnership Example 1
WHY I NEEDED A PARTNER

At the time, I had just lost my job. I had limited capital, and I wasn't able to get approved for a loan because I was technically unemployed. I needed a partner who could get approved for the loan and bring the majority of the capital for the deal I had found.

HOW I FOUND A PARTNER

Before I joined BiggerPockets as the cohost for the *Real Estate Rookie* podcast, I had my own podcast called *Your First Real Estate Investment*. I had a relatively small audience, but through that podcast, I was able to grow my network and meet other aspiring real estate investors.

One of the people that I met had been keeping track of my growing Airbnb portfolio, and they reached out and told me they wanted to partner with me on a future deal. Once I found a deal that I believed made sense, I contacted this person and presented the partnership opportunity to them.

HOW WE STRUCTURED THE PARTNERSHIP

For this deal, we created an equity partnership that included a mix of labor contributions and equity contributions.

I sourced the deal and analyzed it to make sure it hit our return metrics. Then I went out and presented it to an investor who had expressed an interest in partnering with us on a deal.

I brought 25 percent of the capital that was needed to close the deal, and our partner brought the remaining 75 percent of the capital. When it came to equity and profit sharing, we decided to make those numbers match our capital contributions. Our partner kept 75 percent ownership of the property and would receive 75 percent of the profits each month, and I kept 25 percent ownership of the property and would receive 25 percent of the profits every month.

In addition to sourcing the deal, I set the property up (which is a lot of work when it's an Airbnb) and I manage the property on a day-to-day basis. To compensate myself for this daily work, I get paid a 15 percent property management fee. My total monthly payments from this partnership are 25 percent of the cash flow *plus* 15 percent of gross revenue.

Since we each contributed capital toward the deal, there was no capital recapture in place. And once the property sells, I'll take 25 percent and my partner will take 75 percent.

Ashley's Partnership Example 2
HOW I FOUND A PARTNER

After a couple years of investing with Scott, I met another investor, who we'll call Joe. Joe was a friend of a friend. We somehow started talking about real estate one day. Joe had one investment property of his own and wanted to buy more. We started researching a new market and each of us bought a duplex in that area. This was the first property I had bought on my own without a partner, and the same for him. After many months of conversation and watching each other go through the acquisition, rehab, and renting of our new duplexes, we decided to partner on our first deal.

We didn't jump right into a deal; we took our time getting to know each other and what strengths and weaknesses we would each bring to the table. It was about a year after that initial real estate conversation that we closed on our first property. That initial conversation was, of course, full of dreams of building this huge empire together, but we started out with one property under one LLC. We took my kids' names and his dogs' names and used their initials to create our LLC. That's always a fun part—creating the name for the LLC, especially if no one will see it except maybe your tenants, your attorney, and your loan officer when it's on a rental property. One of my other LLCs is actually a *Tommy Boy* reference!

HOW WE STRUCTURED THE PARTNERSHIP

We got a property under contract first, then created the LLC. We used the same partnership agreement that I had used with my first partner. My attorney had given me a Word document instead of a PDF, so I was able to go in and make changes. I saved so much time and money because I didn't need to have my attorney create a brand-new agreement for us. I changed what needed to be done, then gave it to my attorney for a final glance. Our operating agreement gave us each 50 percent equity, 50 percent cash flow, and 50 percent of the responsibility. I would oversee the property management, leasing, financing, and acquisition. Joe would handle maintenance, turnovers, project management, and estimating rehabs.

The best part of this partnership was that there was always the understanding that it would never actually be 50/50. There would be months where I'd be taking on the majority of the workload and vice versa. If I learned one thing from this partnership, it was that if you don't have this understanding going into it, then you should set some expectations. You don't want to be in the position where partners are pointing fingers and saying, "It's not fair."

Joe and I would eagerly pick up each other's slack when needed because it was never assumed that one person would do the other person's job. We both wanted the best for our investment, and sometimes that meant leaning on each other.

I think being friends before partners helped this aspect. There were moments when we weren't perfect and had disputes. We had no written agreement on how to resolve these issues. Going forward, a plan for resolutions is something any investor should have in place. It's impossible to predict every scenario that may occur or decision that may come up, but plan for as many as possible—now and in the future. Plan for the things you never could have anticipated and have a decision-maker rule in your partnership agreement. A decision-maker rule will break the tie for any decisions that aren't agreed upon. There are two common examples of how to deal with this: The first is to consult a trusted third person who is not involved in the business. This could be a trusted, respected, and unbiased person in your industry (mutually agreed upon) or a business coach or consultant. The second option is to clearly determine what each person's department of control and decision is. For example, Ashley has final say in property management and acquisition (sourcing deals, analyzing, funding, and getting under contract). Tony has final say in maintenance, capital improvements, and exit of property (buy and hold, flip, etc).

CHANGING THE OWNERSHIP

We maintained the 50/50 LLC for several deals and then transitioned to a new partnership where I was 60 percent owner, and he was 40 percent owner. We did this by creating a new LLC. The current properties stayed in our existing LLC, and any new properties would go into whichever LLC was fitting. The reason we did the 60 percent to me in the new LLC was because I was going to be putting more money into the deal, and I had acquired the deal. Joe also knew the time he was putting into this deal would be limited. We both agreed on this, and it was something we had discussed.

When creating a partnership, take it deal by deal. There is no reason to commit to every deal with the same structure or even the same partner.

Tony's Partnership Example 2
WHY WE NEEDED A PARTNER

The property we wanted was an off-market deal, but it was being sold as part of a package of three properties. The seller was willing to work with us only if we were able to close on all three. We had limited capital and didn't have the ability to carry three mortgages, so we had to reach out to our network to find a potential partner who was interested in the off-market property and had the ability to purchase the home.

HOW WE FOUND A PARTNER

By the time we found this deal, we had set up a website for our real estate company, and we made it super easy for people to submit their contact information and let us know if they were interested in partnering with us.

So once we found this deal, we already had a small database of potential partners. We then presented that deal to all of the partners and went with the first one who agreed to our terms.

Again, this goes back to Chapter 3. As you increase the number of people who know you, like you, and trust you, the easier it becomes to find potential partners.

HOW WE STRUCTURED THE PARTNERSHIP

For this deal, we created an equity partnership that included a mix of labor contributions and equity contributions.

Just like the previous property, this was an off-market deal that I sourced and analyzed to make sure it hit our return metrics. Then I presented it to an investor who had expressed an interest in partnering with us on a deal.

For this property, our partner contributed 100 percent of the capital that was needed to cover the down payment, closing costs, and start-up costs. We decided to split equity and profits right down the middle, with each of us getting 50 percent.

For this deal, I did not receive a property management fee. I was compensated for my property management work through the 50 percent profit share I received.

There was also no capital recapture in place, so once the property sells, I'll take 50 percent and the partner will take 50 percent.

Ashley's Partnership Example 3
HOW I FOUND A PARTNER

My sister graduated college in May, started her first job in August, and needed a place to live. At this time I was looking to buy another property, and my sister's job was two minutes away from one of my other rentals. I loved the area and it had really appreciated over the years.

There was a house in the area that had been on the market for over ninety days. The issue was that both tenants were on long-term leases and low rents. I had toured the house when it was first listed, and the seller contacted my agent saying the lower unit would terminate their lease early if the property sold.

HOW WE STRUCTURED THE PARTNERSHIP

Our idea was that I would gift my sister the money she needed for the house, and I would be 50 percent owner on the deed; in exchange, she would get the opportunity to make it her primary residence and get an FHA loan—low money down and low interest.

A lot of people told us if I was on the deed, I had to be on the mortgage. Not true! If my sister defaulted, I'd obviously lose my interest in the house to the bank, but I didn't have a personal responsibility for the mortgage. My debt-to-income ratio was not affected.

When my sister decided to move out, we split the cash flow and eventually split the proceeds from the sale. She was able to buy a house with no money out of her pocket, and I was able to get ownership in a house with only a 3.5 percent down payment instead of a 20 percent down payment.

This partnership worked out for both of us. It gave her equity in a property and immediate low-cost housing ($45 a month!), and it gave me equity in the property with some long-term play of eventual cash flow and appreciation.

As we've said, there are so many creative ways to structure a partnership. In this case we were very clear with the bank that this was how we were structuring the deal. They knew I was gifting the money and that I was going on the deed. The last thing you want to do is commit mortgage fraud.

Tony's Partnership Example 3
HOW WE STRUCTURED THE PARTNERSHIP

Just like the previous two properties, this deal was an equity partnership that included a mix of labor contributions and equity contributions.

We actually sourced this deal off of the MLS and were able to negotiate the price down to a number that allowed us to hit our specific return metrics.

Our partner brought 100 percent of the capital, and they carried the mortgage. For this deal, we gave our partner 60 percent of the equity and cash flow, and we kept 40 percent. There is no property management fee, as our 40 percent profit share covers my compensation as the property manager.

Since our partner brought 100 percent of the capital, and it was a relatively large amount of money, we decided to include a capital recapture. When the property sells, our partner will recoup their initial investment first, and then the remaining amount will be split 60/40.

Ashley's Partnership Example 4
WHY I NEEDED A PARTNER

I was in a transition period in my real estate business. I had handed my long-term rentals over to a property manager, sold a couple of the low-performing ones, and wanted to venture into something new. I felt my long-term buy and hold portfolio was stable and a strong foundation for trying something I hadn't done before.

I had experience with rehabs and wanted to continue to do them. I wanted to increase the workload that I could take on so I could scale my business.

I could have hired someone, but at this time in my life, I wanted a partner instead of an employee. There's a difference between someone who has ownership in a property and someone who is just being paid. I wanted a person who was loyal and willing to work for that equity and to share the responsibility. Also, I think I work better when I have someone to bounce ideas off and brainstorm with. Going into this new chapter of my investing, I wanted all of those things in a partner.

I also learned over the years how important it is to find a partner who complements your strengths and weaknesses. During this time, I started taking inventory of both of these, and also what I *didn't* want to do.

HOW I FOUND A PARTNER

My cousin invited me on her friend Daryl's boat, and he became my next business partner. Over the summer we talked periodically about real estate investing. We also discussed how he was unhappy with his current job as a construction foreman. He wasn't building wealth and felt stuck in a lifestyle he didn't want. I knew that his skill set was something I could really benefit from, both in terms of managing the rehabs for me and communicating with the contractors. As time went on, there were many other benefits that I learned would be an advantage to both of us.

The first time we met was in June. We started seriously talking about investing together in September and began to get properties under contract in November and December.

HOW WE STRUCTURED THE PARTNERSHIP

We structured this partnership 50/50, splitting the roles and responsibilities. It started with Daryl generating the leads, then I would analyze and make the offers. Finding the funds to purchase the properties was up to me too. We shared the responsibility of due diligence when under contract. Once we closed, Daryl took over with the rehabs.

I wish I could say I stayed out of it and let him run with it, but I interjected a lot, which taught many lessons and created learning experiences for us both. We also set the expectation that Daryl might do some of the actual labor for the rehabs. This was something we decided we would play by ear, and it did end up happening. In those situations, we would discuss if an additional draw would be paid to Daryl for performing labor. (So far, we haven't come up with a situation where we've decided to pay out. We have found it still fair and within Daryl's scope to perform some of the work on the properties.)

Once the property was done, I would handle the refinance and get it listed.

We created a separate LLC different from my other ones. This one has us both listed as members with 50 percent ownership each. We have an operating agreement in place. If one of us decides to put money into the LLC, then that person is paid an interest rate for their money (below market rate, of course).

A NEW STRATEGY

A new strategy we focused on was buying land with cabins. We bought old, run-down cabins on beautiful parcels ranging from three acres to thirty acres. We renovated the cabins into something modern with a lot of focus on the bathrooms and kitchens, not skimping on the tile or cabinets.

These properties were going to be short-term rentals. I had one short-term rental arbitrage (where you lease a property from someone else and legally rent it out on sites like Airbnb as a short-term rental), but this was the first time owning the property and having more than one. We needed to build out the operations, but we hadn't really discussed who would be in charge of that. One mistake we made was not being clear on that when we first partnered. It worked out well because we just decided to outsource. We hired someone to create our short-term rental operation and run it. We invested the money instead of investing the time to research and set it up.

Having a partner who not only complements your strengths and weaknesses but is also like-minded can create a smoother experience when you do hit bumps in the road.

Making Amendments

These are a few examples of the ways you can structure partnerships, but there are many different options. Some of our examples may be applicable to you, others may not be what you want. We want you to build and tailor a relationship to work for you and your partners.

As you move forward with your partnership, remember that it may not be built out perfectly—something we learned throughout our partnerships. Who knows if there even is a "perfect" partnership structure? Keep the option open to amend your partnership as needed. Don't get stuck in something long-term that is no longer worth your while.

Partnership structures can adapt and pivot over time. It all comes with the growing pains of building a business.

Chapter 8
ADDITIONAL AGREEMENTS FOR ANY PARTNERSHIP

— *Ashley* —

A real estate partnership agreement isn't only about outlining the structure; there are other clauses or agreements that should be considered as well.

The material we will discuss in this chapter can be included in the partnership agreement or as an additional agreement. These are not necessary to legally form a partnership, but they are highly recommended as ways to add more layers of protection for you and your partners.

As we have discussed previously, there are limitless decisions and scenarios that will come up during your partnership, and all you can do is plan how to handle as many as you can think of, or at least the ones that most commonly occur.

Have you ever gone through your insurance policy? Have you actually read all of the things it will or won't cover? Keep this in mind when building your agreements. No one ever expects to have their house catch fire, a tree fall on it, a sump pump fail, a pipe to burst, or termites eating the studs. You hope that none of that happens, but if it does, you know you are protected and won't have to pay out of pocket. Unless, of course, your policy doesn't cover one of those incidents, in which case you've hopefully got some cash reserves!

There is no such thing as being too prepared for every situation that could happen. For any scenario you think could possibly occur, write down how it will be handled or what the outcome could be.

A big part of this will include forecasting possible outcomes of your partnership and providing options when those things do occur. It may even get a little morbid, but we are here to face reality and be prepared for it.

Bonus Content to Your Agreement

The three bonus items we want to cover include a buy-sell agreement, life insurance policies, and shotgun clauses.

A buy-sell agreement breaks down what happens if one or both of you decide to sell the property or ownership interest in the business. Life insurance policies provide a safety net in the event of one partner's death, which benefits the surviving partner and the family of the deceased partner. Lastly, the shotgun clause is put in place to force another partner out of their ownership interest.

Did that last one get your mind spinning? What would be the reasons for this? We'll go into that and more in this chapter.

As someone eager to start a new partnership, you may be tempted to overlook some of these "bonus items" for your partnership agreement. Maybe you're excited and anxious to get the ball rolling, or you just can't stand semantics, paperwork, and dragging things out. It may take more work, negotiating, and time up front to add these items, but it will save you from having to do those things in the future when even just one scenario comes up.

Buy-Sell Agreement

The buy-sell agreement should coincide with the operating agreement. The buy-sell agreement states what happens if one or more of the partners decide they want to sell. It can also state a time when the partners will consider selling and how they will decide if they are going to sell. In each situation, it could be just one partner selling their ownership interest, selling just a property, or selling a company as a whole. This can all be integrated into your operating agreement or could be a separate agreement.

EXPIRATION DATE

The first thing you want to consider when negotiating the buy-sell agreement is if there is going to be a time frame for a discussion regarding selling. In Tony's joint venture agreements, he puts an expiration date of five years on the contract. He does this for each property. At the five-year mark, the partners sit down and vote on whether they want to sell or not. If both partners, or even just one partner, want to sell, then the property is put up for sale. If neither partner wants to sell, then the property is not sold. At this point, there are several different options and variations to consider. If one partner wants to sell, you could include the option for right of first refusal.

VALUATION

Right of first refusal is when someone legally has a claim to purchase your property when you decide to sell. This doesn't entitle them to pay any price they want; it states that they must pay what you are asking for the property or match the highest offer. You could add a formula that determines a price that is part of the buy-sell agreement. An attorney or CPA could help you determine a formula that would project the future value of the business or property. Of course, we can't predict where the market will be when it's time to sell, but this could be used as a base.

An example of a formula would be multiplying the income before any tax, depreciation, and amortization by a specified number. This is typically used to find the value of a business.

Another factor that may come into play is the book value of the business or property. This would be the assets minus the liabilities—for example, the value of your property minus the liabilities, which is the owner's equity. Keep in mind that the book value only takes into account what is on your books, so this would be what you purchased the property for as well as any capital improvements you made for the property that are added into the assets. Your liabilities would be any debt that is accrued for that property. Again, these valuations are mostly used for businesses. If you have a business and not just one property for which you are creating a buy-sell agreement, then those formulas are something to consider.

Below is an example of a start of a buy-sell agreement.

THE REMINGTON COMPANY
BUY-SELL AGREEMENT

THIS AGREEMENT, effective as of May 1, 2023, is made by and between The Remington Company, a domestic corporation having its principal place of business at 150 Lundy's Lane, Springville, NY 14034 (hereinafter referred to as the "Corporation"), Ashley Hoffman, residing at 790 Compound Road, Boston, NY 14075, and Evan Edwards, residing at 94 Mirandez Road, Boston, NY 14075 (herein collectively referred to as the "Shareholders"), all of whom are collectively referred to as the "Parties."

WHEREAS, the Corporation is capitalized as follows: 150 shares of preferred stock and fifty shares of common stock; and

WHEREAS, as of the date of this Agreement, Ashley Hoffman owns 43.6 shares of the common stock of the Corporation, or 87.2 percent of the common stock of the Corporation; and

WHEREAS, as of the date of this Agreement, Evan Edwards owns 6.4 shares of the common stock, or 12.8 percent of the common stock of the Corporation; and

WHEREAS, it is believed by the Parties that it is in their best interests as well as the best interests of the Corporation to restrict the future transfer of shares of common stock of the Corporation and to outline a plan for the gradual purchase of common stock by Ashley Hoffman from Evan Edwards or the Corporation, as the case may be.

NOW, THEREFORE, in consideration of the foregoing and of the mutual promises contained herein, the sufficiency of which is hereby acknowledged, the parties agree as follows:

1. Restriction on Transfers. Except as expressly otherwise permitted by the Agreement no Shareholder may pledge, sell, or transfer any of the shares of common stock of the Corporation, and any attempted pledge, sale, or transfer not so permitted shall be void and without effect.

2. Valuation of Shares. The Shareholders agree that, as of the date of this Agreement, the valuation of the common stock is ONE MILLION DOLLARS ($1,000,000.00), or $20,000.00 per share. The Shareholders shall annually set a value for the common stock of the Corporation by vote and shall make a record of such value by executing a certificate of valuation. The most recent certificate of valuation, duly executed by the parties, shall supersede all prior certificates of valuation. The fair value of each share as redetermined from time to time shall take into account the tangible and intangible assets of the Corporation, and other relevant factors, including liabilities of the Corporation. Goodwill shall be deemed to be of no value unless actually paid for and carried on the books of the Corporation as an asset. In the event that no value for the Corporation has been established and recorded within eighteen (18) months prior to the date of determination under this Agreement, then the Shareholders agree that a reasonable valuation shall be an annual escalation of five percent (5%).

THE SEVEN

There are seven main elements of any contract: the offer, acceptance, consideration, intention to create legal relations, authority and capacity, and certainty.

Notice the elements of the buy-sell agreement above. I want you to pay special attention to the consideration piece. This is under "2. Valuation of Shares." There is a set formula to figure out the purchase price. As of the date of the agreement, if Evan were to purchase shares, he could buy them at $20,000 per share. If Evan waits one calendar year from the execution of the agreement, he will have to pay $21,000 per share ($20,000 × 5%). According to the buy-sell, the valuation will continue to increase by 5 percent each year. This is in anticipation that the company will be growing in value. When you are creating this kind of buyout, be sure to put a start date. In this example, the start date was immediate. Any time I wanted to sell shares, Evan could buy them.

A CPA and/or your attorney can assist in creating a valuation formula for the agreement that states what the shares will be sold for if a partner decides to buy out another partner. Having multiple exit strategies if one partner wants out is important, so be sure to include not only the process of buying from each other, but also selling to a third party. In my example above, the partners are limited to only selling to each other. This is completely up to you and your partner. Personally, I don't want to suddenly find out one day that I'm partnered with a stranger because Evan sold his ownership interest to him.

Specifically state when interest can be sold, who it can be sold to, and how much it can be sold for. If both partners agree that a partner can sell their shares at any time, or maybe later on both partners agree that one can sell their shares to a third party, you might not want to use the valuation and instead try to get market price for the shares.

Setting a valuation, or a way to determine purchase price, provides protection and makes it clear to both parties what is expected in the course of the sale. If the partners both decide they want to sell, then the agreement could state that the property will be sold for market price—for example, what it will sell for on the open market.

There should also be some language in the buy-sell around accepting and declining offers. What happens if the property sits on the market for ninety days and isn't selling at your asking price? This should be outlined in the agreement, stating whether one member is the deciding factor or if you keep the property. Just like in your operating agreement, there should be a way to mediate this decision that is laid out in writing.

Last thing on the buy-sell agreement: It is negotiable. It can be changed or amended if both parties agree. Maybe you listened to a podcast and heard someone discuss one thing they included in their buy-sell, and you decide you should add it to yours. Every year, during your annual meeting, review all of your agreements. You may find things that need to be changed or, more likely, specifics that need to be added.

Partner's Death

Here is where we get to the morbid part. You or your partner could pass away. We know, it's awful to think about, but just like everything else in your operating agreement, we need to consider all possible scenarios.

Have you ever thought about what would happen in the event of your partner's death? In most cases their heir (usually their spouse or kids), would become your new partner. Do you want that? Maybe, maybe not. Your answer today may be different from your answer three years from now.

Let's break down some options. The first option after your partner passes away is selling the property, the proceeds of which you and your partner's heir would receive. You could then buy the ownership interest from the heir and own 100 percent of the company. Here we are again at buying out a partner, obviously for a different reason than just a desire on their part to sell. You would be purchasing from your partner's heir. Different factors and variables could come into play. It's best to have this scenario planned out.

For our example, let's say each partner is 50 percent owner. If you have significantly grown your portfolio, which has a lot of equity, but you're also continuously shelling out money for new deals, then how could you afford to buy out your partner's heir? The last thing you want to do is save a chunk of money that is making little to no interest because you're anticipating the demise of your partner. You want to have that money working for you! Your option is to turn to life insurance.

LIFE INSURANCE

You and your partner can get a life insurance policy on each other with the business as owner of the policy. You are the beneficiary, and your partner is the insured, and vice versa for the policy your partner has on you. The business can expense the cost of the policy premium since the business is the owner of the policy. The life insurance policy proceeds would be used by the surviving partner to buy the shares from the partner's heirs. The business would now be owned by the surviving partner, and the heirs would walk away with a lump sum of money. This hopefully appeases everyone, given the circumstances.

Shotgun Clause

Unfortunately, there may be a situation in which you have to force your partner out of the business. There are so many different reasons that you may no longer want to be involved in a partnership. You, of course, have the option to leave the business yourself, but it can be hard leaving the blood, sweat, and tears you put in to build it.

As you have probably learned as an investor, there is a long-term play to owning property. If you had to sell your stake in the business, you would most likely get a payout, but then you'd lose all the benefits that real estate investing brings long-term, such as the tax advantages, appreciation, and possibly the active or passive income that comes with your business. In a scenario where you want to keep the business but force your partner out, it must be for good reason—and that reason needs to be outlined in the partnership agreement, where it is referred to as the "shotgun clause." The partner is forced out without their consent.

ILLEGAL ACTIVITY

If your partner is hurting the company financially or even morally (such as harassment), you won't want them involved anymore, and it may be difficult to convince them to leave on their own. Of course, a partner might be embarrassed and leave on their own, but if that doesn't happen, you will have to force them out.

A common reason your partner may be asked to leave the company is illegal activity. This could be outlined as illegal activity that is directly correlated with the business operation or an illegal act that had nothing to do with the normal course of business. Examples of the former could be stealing money from the company, engaging in gambling with company funds, fraud, or harassment of employees. Every scenario doesn't need to be listed in the shotgun clause, but it can be spelled out for extra peace of mind. You can use language that your attorney provides you that is all-encompassing.

In the shotgun clause, you can also state that illegal activity is grounds for forcing out even if the person commits a criminal act or service that doesn't have anything to do with the business. This could be if they commit a crime such as armed robbery, murder, or identity theft. Even if your partner does everything right for your business, the trust and respect of your clients or customers could be lost due to what your partner does outside of the business.

BUSINESS OPERATIONS DISAGREEMENT

Besides your partner doing something illegal, they could be forced out due to a discrepancy in the operation of the business. You or your partner may have a disagreement that can't be resolved. In a situation where there are more than two partners, an additional partner may be forced out. If two partners agree on something and the third partner doesn't, this can lead to a call on the shotgun clause.

COMPENSATION

I do want to stress that if these shotgun clauses are called upon, it doesn't mean your partner is forced to walk away with nothing. There most likely will need to be compensation or some arrangement for you to buy out their shares. This clause will force them to sell, whether it's to you or someone else. Just like we talked about in the buy-sell, you want to make sure you have the right of first refusal. You don't want a spiteful, vengeful partner picking out who your new partner may be.

IT'S NOT THEIR FAULT

We've made the shotgun clause scenarios sound as though your partner has turned into a horrible person, but there are also circumstances that could happen that are out of your partner's control. If your partner is in a terrible accident or diagnosed with a disease or an illness that renders them unable to fulfill their duties, you may need to enact the clause.

If you didn't listen to our prior advice and create a buy-sell agreement with your partner and they passed away, you may need to call on the shotgun clause again. In this situation, maybe the wife wants to be partners with you now that she has inherited the shares from her deceased husband. She may have ulterior motives for the business. At this time, you'd have to enforce the shotgun clause to get her out.

LAST RESORT

The shotgun clause should be a last resort, enacted only if negotiation or mediation isn't working. Just a friendly reminder: If all of this can happen to your partner, then it can happen to you! There should be clear expectations in the shotgun clause as to what can and can't happen. Keep the clause in mind so you aren't blindsided when you are served legal papers that your partners are forcing you out.

There are also disadvantages to having a shotgun clause, including the difficulty of creating a valuation of what the shares should be purchased for upon the forced sale.

Protect Yourself

The start of a new partnership is like being in a new relationship or marriage: there's always a honeymoon period. Everything feels so warm and fuzzy, you have a glow about you, and you can't imagine life without each other. Yet, people change, the market changes, lives change, and these variables can cause all sorts of problems, emotions, and turmoil.

Don't get us wrong—they can also cause partnerships to expand and become better, but why put yourself at risk of something bad happening? Your partnership will be more solid if each partner feels safe and protected in their investments of time and money.

REAL-LIFE PARTNERSHIPS
Oscar Yerena
INVESTS IN: Tennessee

I have two real estate partners. My first partner was there for my very first deal, and we went 50/50 on all cash and profits. I brought the deal, which I found on the MLS, and my partner brought the knowledge to analyze the inspection report and the repairs. We're located in different areas of California but invested in Tennessee, so we were both out-of-state investors.

My second partner is located in Tennessee and was actually the Realtor for my first deal. We spoke about my game plan for investing, and she expressed an interest in partnering on future deals. She and I have two single-family homes together. Our partnership is also 50/50, with both of us going 50/50 on cost and profits. She brought both deals to the table (both off-market, the first with seller financing and the second all-cash) and partnered with me to split the risk and bring someone in with a bit more investing knowledge. It helps me to have her as my eyes and ears in the area, especially since she's an agent and has boots-on-the-ground connections.

Chapter 9
COMMUNICATION IS KEY

— Tony —

The most important part of any relationship (friendly, romantic, or business) is communication. You can almost always gauge the health of a relationship by the quality of the communication within that relationship.

Your real estate partnership is no different.

If you and your partner are not communicating with each other, you're sending yourselves down a dangerous road.

But if you and your partner can foster a healthy level of communication in the relationship, then you significantly increase your chances of having a successful partnership. Because here's the truth: You and your partner will certainly have instances of disagreement. You'll probably have a handful of situations where you're completely annoyed with each other. And there'll be plenty of times when you're frustrated or upset.

But if you and your partner can communicate well, then all of those issues become easier to deal with. Over the course of this chapter, we'll break down why communication is so important and give you tactical steps you can take to keep the quality of communication high.

Systems for Effective Partner Communication

The word "system" is defined by the Oxford English Dictionary as "a set of principles or procedures according to which something is done; an organized framework or method." And every single real estate partnership needs a system for managing communication. You and your partner need an "organized framework" to help facilitate meaningful conversation and manage conflict in a healthy way.

Over the next few pages, we'll break down the systems you should have in your partnership to make sure you and your partner are always on the same page. This information is extremely useful in any type of relationship, whether it's with a significant other, a vendor, a coworker, a boss, or a tenant. Effective communication can lead to clarity and effectiveness in all areas of your life.

THE ISSUES LIST

Every business that's ever existed has had issues that prevented it from running at 100 percent efficiency. There's always something within the business that "isn't quite right." Or there are those lingering problems that everyone is aware of, but because the pain isn't too severe, people come to live with the problem.

Part of what makes a real estate partnership successful (or any business partnership, for that matter) is that partnership's ability to identify issues in the business and work together to solve them. The bad news is that most people haven't created a process to systematically identify and fix issues within their businesses. Luckily, there's a solution that's relatively easy to implement.

In his book *Traction,* author Gino Wickman explains his framework for how a business should operate. He calls it the Entrepreneurial Operating System (EOS). It's an incredible book on managing processes and progression toward the accomplishment of goals, as well as the people who are responsible for those goals.

A key component of EOS is called the Issues List, and it applies incredibly well to real estate partnerships.

Think of your Issues List as the database for all the issues that exist in the business that are preventing you from achieving your business goals. It's a living, breathing document that changes and grows with your business. As you or your partner find things that are broken—processes that aren't running smoothly, responsibilities that aren't met, metrics that aren't meeting expectations—you add those things to the Issues List so you can fix them.

The Issues List is a great tool for communication because it keeps you and your partner on the same page about what the actual problems are in the partnership and helps facilitate healthy discussions around how those issues should be resolved.

What Do Issues Have to Do with Real Estate Partnerships?

Why are we talking about the Issues List in a chapter that's supposed to be about communication? The simple truth is that one of the most important things you and your partner should be talking about are the issues that exist in your real estate partnership.

The issues could be related to the property that you've invested in together. Maybe your tenants are constantly late paying rent in your long-term rental. Maybe your contractors are constantly missing deadlines at your flip. Maybe the guests at your short-term rental keep complaining about the check-in process. Maybe the cold-callers you've hired from your wholesaling business aren't booking any appointments.

Or perhaps the issues are related to the actual partnership itself. Maybe before the partnership started, you both assumed that you'd be splitting management duties equally, but after a few months, it becomes clear that one person is carrying a heavier workload. Maybe one partner is enthusiastic about the duties they committed to but they aren't necessarily effective.

The list of possibilities is endless. The point is that you need to document the issues that exist within your partnership and to discuss those issues regularly.

REGULAR MEETINGS WITH YOUR PARTNER

We've already talked about *why* communication is so important with your partner, but now let's talk about the right *cadence* for communicating with your partner. One thing to call out is that the right cadence for a partnership is going to vary depending on the roles that each partner plays.

Remember, there are two key types of real estate partnerships: equity partnerships and debt partnerships. And even within those partnerships, there are several ways that a person can contribute: property management, rehab, bookkeeping and accounting, deal finding, deal analysis, capital, and carrying the mortgage, to name a few.

Say, for example, that you've entered into a debt partnership where you are the lender, and the other partner is the borrower. In this situation, it may not be necessary for you and your partner to meet on a regular basis. All that matters to you is that you're repaid your money by the date and time that your agreement states. You don't need to check in with the borrower to see how the project is going. You don't need to get status updates on when the material is getting delivered to the rehab site. All you need to know is whether your payments are being sent out on time.

In my own debt partnerships for our rehab projects, I speak with my partners once right before the deal closes to complete all of the necessary paperwork. We'll speak again once the rehab is complete, and we're listing the property for sale. And the last time we speak is when the deal closes, and I congratulate them on their passive return.

That's it.

And it works because the entire reason they signed up for the partnership was because they wanted a passive role. They don't want to be involved in the day-to-day management of the project.

In my main real estate partnership, my partner and I own thirty properties together. And we both play an active role in managing that portfolio on a daily basis. We have a formal meeting every week, and we speak informally almost daily; that's the level of communication we need to maintain an effective partnership. Even if you are speaking every day, it can be extremely valuable to have a meeting set aside, whether that be each week or each month, to touch base with an agenda and dedicated time to discussing issues in-depth.

Look at the different roles that each partner is playing: The more each partner is integrated into the day-to-day work of running the real estate business, the more frequently you should be meeting. The less integrated a partner is, the less often you need to meet.

With that in mind, let's talk through the cadence that my partners and I follow in our business: quarterly and annual planning meetings and weekly tactical meetings.

Quarterly and Annual Planning Meetings

One of the most important conversations you and your partner will have will be about the future direction of your real estate partnership and the business that you are building together. Let me say this as loudly and as clearly as possible: *There's a very real likelihood that at some point, your goals and your partner's goals will no longer align.* And if that happens, it may be a sign that the partnership needs to radically change, or possibly end altogether. But the *only* way you'll recognize this is if you and your partner are regularly communicating about your goals and vision for the partnership.

As we discussed in Chapter 5, an important part of keeping aligned with your partner is having a regular cadence to talk about long-term plans. We recommend that you have these strategic conversations on a quarterly and annual basis. The purpose of the quarterly meeting is to make sure you're on track for your yearly goals. The purpose of the annual meeting is to recalibrate, review last year's goals, and get aligned on the goals for this year.

We won't harp on that again. The only point in mentioning it here is that a critical part of keeping your partnership aligned is meeting on a regular basis to talk about the partnership at a strategic level. Again, put into your operating agreement that these alignment meetings are mandatory at these times throughout the life of the partnership.

Weekly Tactical Meetings

Once you've established your annual and quarterly goals, it's critically important that you and your partner are meeting regularly; I'm a big fan of the weekly meeting.

While the annual planning and quarterly planning meetings are focused on long-term goals and strategies, the weekly meetings are about the activities and obstacles associated with those goals and strategies. This meeting is focused on the nitty-gritty.

There are countless books on the topic of running effective meetings, and it's not within the scope of this book to teach that concept in detail. Again, *Traction* by Gino Wickman does a fantastic job outlining the agenda for a productive weekly meeting.

Just make sure that when you and your partner meet, you're reviewing the metrics and you're holding each other accountable to completing the action items that each of you committed to finishing. This is also the time when you should be working through any items present on your Issues List.

Staying in Your Lane

One of the most difficult parts of being in a real estate partnership can be trusting your partner to hold up their end of the bargain, which is understandable. Maybe this is your first real estate investment ever, and you're concerned about whether or not this whole real estate investing thing actually works. And to ease those concerns, you feel compelled to triple-check and quadruple-check what's being done at every step of the way.

But there's one important thing to remember: You partnered with this person for a reason. In Chapter 2, we discussed the different ways that a person can bring value to a partnership. As you read through that chapter, hopefully you were able to identify the value that you're able to bring to a partnership but also identify the value that a potential partner could bring to you.

In Chapter 3, we encouraged you to take your time in finding a partner. And in Chapter 6, we outlined the different roles that each partner should play based on their unique strengths and weaknesses.

If you've taken our advice so far in this book, it means that you've identified exactly what skills and abilities you can bring to a partnership, *and* you've identified what skills and abilities you need your partner to bring. And, more often than not, it means your partner is going to be doing the activities that you don't have the time, desire, or ability to do yourself.

The truth is, you are doing yourself and your partner a disservice if you constantly try to interfere in the work that your partner is doing.

Let's say, for example, that you and your partner decide to flip a house together. Since you're great with numbers and have tons of friends who are real estate agents, you take charge of acquisitions. And since your partner is great at managing budgets and is a project manager in their day job, they take charge of managing the rehab.

After a few weeks of hard work, you finally find a property that meets your criteria. You and your partner close on that property thirty days later. Now the baton passes to your partner. You set up a weekly sync to keep tabs on the project. Every week, your partner comes to the meeting with a crystal clear project update. They provide timelines for completion and updated budgets. They clearly communicate the issues that are popping up, and the two of you work together to problem-solve those issues.

But say, unbeknownst to your partner, you were *also* communicating with the subcontractors who were working the job. And after your partner gave them directions to replace the cabinets with new cabinets, you gave them directions to keep the cabinets and restain them.

Or say that your partner chose "Agreeable Gray" from Sherwin-Williams as the paint color, but after walking the property yourself, you decided that you like "Accessible Beige."

How do you think your partner would feel knowing that you were going behind them and "correcting" all of their work? Furthermore, what makes you think that your decisions are any better? What if your partner did their research, looked at all of the comparable sales for the property, and realized that properties with Agreeable Gray and new cabinets sold for 15 percent more?

If you partnered with someone for their skills and abilities, then trust them to perform.

Use your weekly meetings and Issues List as your mechanism to make sure your partner is holding up their end of the bargain and performing their duties at a high level. Otherwise, get out of the way and let them do their job.

Awkward Conversations

It wouldn't be a chapter about partnership communication without bringing up the elephant in the room. Sometimes, being in a real estate partnership means you and your partner need to have some awkward conversations.

WHY YOU NEED TO HAVE AWKWARD CONVERSATIONS

Avoiding difficult or awkward conversations is the easy way out for many people. But allowing an issue to exist and grow within your partnership without actively working to resolve it will almost certainly lead to feelings of resentment, frustration, and anger from one or both of you.

Avoiding difficult conversations may seem like a way to keep the peace in the short-term, but it has devastating effects over the long-term. And if one partner starts to resent the other partner, it can lead the partnership down a path of no return where the only option is to end the partnership altogether. Perhaps the partnership could've been saved had everyone just sat down and discussed the issues.

Aside from making you go crazy, not addressing your feelings directly with your partner also leaves them in the dark. When you create a partnership with someone, you and your partner both create expectations of one another. Sometimes those expectations are stated clearly, other times those expectations were never actually communicated. Sometimes you don't even realize you *have* an expectation of your partner until you start to feel that they're not meeting that expectation.

And this is where problems arise.

You could have a situation where your partner's poor performance isn't because they aren't capable or willing. Instead, it's simply because you each entered the partnership with different expectations. Say, for example, your partner's role is to manage the contractors for your rehab, and you expected that they would be at the property every single day. But their expectation of themselves was that they would only need to go once per week.

On the flip side of this example, say you're the partner who signed up to manage the rehab, and your partner is on the other end, frustrated with you because you're not visiting the project enough. Yet, in your mind, you feel like the project is moving along as well as a rehab project can. Sure, there are some issues, but overall, you feel you're fulfilling your commitment to the partnership. If your partner was unhappy with how you were managing the project, wouldn't you want to be told?

Who's in the wrong here? Is your partner wrong for expecting you to be there every single day, or are you in the wrong for not being committed enough? Honestly, it doesn't really matter. You both need to express your frustrations so you can talk through what's reasonable and set clear expectations for how the partnership will move forward.

WHEN YOU NEED TO HAVE AWKWARD CONVERSATIONS

Now that you understand *why* having those tough conversations in your partnership is essential, let's examine some of the instances that require those conversations. Countless reasons could trigger the need for a tough conversation, but they generally fall into one of the following four categories:

Awkward Conversation #1: Partner Isn't Fulfilling Their Duties

Recall from Chapter 6 our discussion on partnership structure. In that chapter, we outlined the different ways each partner can contribute to the partnership, sometimes with their labor, other times with their capital. And as part of creating the structure for your partnership, you should've outlined what role each partner will play.

But what happens when one partner isn't carrying their weight?

Say, for example, you chose the role of deal finder while your partner chose the role of deal analyzer. In your role, you're absolutely crushing it. You're finding deal after deal after deal. You're thrilled that there's so much opportunity for your partnership. The problem is, once the deal hits the desk of your partner, it doesn't go any further. Your partner just can't keep up with the volume of deals that you're finding, and eventually, they just stop analyzing deals altogether. Every time you ask for an update, they give you one excuse or another as to why they haven't analyzed the deals you sent in the last week.

This is a very real possibility. And if you're the partner who is putting in all of the hard work, and the other half of your partnership is literally doing nothing (or close to nothing), you'll find yourself feeling frustrated and upset.

Awkward Conversation #2: Workload Is Not Balanced

Category two is when one partner is putting more work into the partnership, even though the plan was for the workload to be balanced. This may sound similar to category one, but there are some minor differences that justify it being its own category.

In category one, the driver for frustration was that one partner wasn't fulfilling the duties they committed to. In category two, both partners *are* fulfilling all their original duties to the partnership, but you both miscalculated the amount of work that would go into those duties, leading to one partner spending significantly more time working in the partnership.

For example, say that you and your partner decide to invest in a short-term rental together. Your partner decides to run the "front of house" operations, which include all of the guest communication and listing management. And you decide to run the "back of house," which includes managing your cleaners, handymen, and all maintenance requests. The goal of splitting the workload this way was that both you and your partner would spend a roughly equal amount of time running the property.

After one month of running your short-term rental, you and your partner are both fulfilling your duties. Your partner is giving your guests a world-class experience and solving any issues quickly. You're also solving all maintenance requests as soon as they come in, and you're holding your cleaners to an incredibly high standard.

The problem is that your partner realizes that the amount of time it takes to manage the guests is significantly higher than the amount of time it takes to manage maintenance requests. And although both of you are fulfilling your duties, your partner is working three times as much as you are.

Your partner might not be frustrated by this after one month, but they are definitely feeling somewhat concerned about the imbalance. The danger here is if your partner never says anything to you about the imbalance, that concern quickly becomes frustration and eventually evolves into flat-out anger.

In a situation like this, it's important to address this imbalance quickly.

Awkward Conversation #3: Disagreeing on Direction

The first two types of awkward conversations focused on issues relating to the day-to-day management of the partnership. The next two categories focus on bigger, strategic issues.

Awkward conversation number three is when you and your partner disagree on the direction that the partnership and the business need to take in the future.

Say that you and your partner have been working together successfully for one year, and during that time you purchased several properties together. As you think about the future of your real estate portfolio, you realize that you want to scale more aggressively so you can really maximize the cash flow. And even though scaling more aggressively means you and your partner will both have to invest more time and energy into growing the businesses, you believe it's an investment worth making. Your heart truly wants to build an empire.

When you bring up your plans for empire building to your partner, they aren't excited about it like you are. They've come to realize that they prefer to keep the real estate portfolio small but mighty. Their goal isn't a massive portfolio; they just want enough cash flow to cover their basic living expenses. What's more important to them is maintaining their freedom of time. And they understand that they can't have a massive portfolio *and* complete time freedom.

Now you and your partner find yourselves at a crossroads. One of you wants to move at 100 miles per hour, while the other wants to keep the pace nice and easy.

This happens more often than you think. It's true that you can try to avoid this by having discussions about long-term goals before the partnership starts, but the truth is, priorities shift and goals change. And though your partner *thought* they wanted to build a massive portfolio when you first started, it's totally possible that after a year of doing the work, they realize it's not really what they want.

When you find yourself in this situation, you need to sit down and hash things out. This ties back to the importance of having a regular meeting cadence to talk through goals and visions.

If a regular agenda item for your annual team meeting is to revisit your ten-year plan, and one partner feels that the plan does not represent their desires, it becomes easier to have these discussions. But if you and your partner are no longer aligned on the vision for the partnership, it can quickly lead to those same feelings of frustration we've been talking about.

Awkward Conversation #4: Ending the Partnership

Here's a hard truth: Not all real estate partnerships will last forever. Just because a certain partnership made sense today doesn't mean it will make sense tomorrow. Because of that, there's a chance that you will eventually need to end your partnership.

Usually, the desire to end a partnership comes from one of the first three awkward conversations—one partner isn't carrying their weight, or there's a big disconnect in where each partner wants to take the real estate business. And if those differences can't be resolved, then usually it means that the partnership might need to end.

It doesn't get more awkward than this, especially if the desire to end the partnership is one-sided. But if someone in the partnership wants to end things, then this is by far the most important conversation.

This conversation is harder to bring up, since it'd be a little weird to add "End Partnership" as an agenda item for your weekly meeting. The easiest way to lead into this is by simply saying, "Hey, I've had something on my mind that I wanted to share with you." Take a deep breath and then say your reasoning for wanting to end things.

You'll probably feel some anxiety leading up to the conversation, but if you know it's the right decision, you'll feel a major weight lifted off your shoulders once you're done.

Texts, Phone Calls, and Face-to-Face Conversations

We live in a world where so much of our communication is handled through text messages. And while texting is a super convenient way to have most conversations, it should *not* be used to have any tough conversations with your partner.

When you communicate through text, you don't get the full picture of how the other person is receiving your messages or the true intent behind their messages. When you and your partner communicate through text, you don't get to hear each other's tone of voice or see each other's facial expressions. You can't see each other's body posture or any of the other nonverbal cues that come with talking face-to-face.

Because of this, text messages can oftentimes be misinterpreted, even if the texts are the exact same words you would use in person.

If you and your partner have a disagreement about something and try to resolve it through texting, and it ends with your partner saying OK, you might find yourself overanalyzing that response and feeling confused about whether or not your partner is really "OK."

Avoid all of the uncertainty that comes along with texting. Commit to having tough conversations in person, or, at a minimum, over a Zoom call, so you can still see each other's body language and hear each other's voices.

Putting It All Together

High-quality communication is probably the most important ingredient to making your partnership successful. Throughout this chapter, we outlined several ways you can make sure that your partnership fosters a healthy level of communication within the relationship. With the strategies we shared, you'll be creating a strong foundation so that as issues arise, you and your partner can work through them effectively.

REAL-LIFE PARTNERSHIPS
Caleb Drake
INVESTS IN: Indiana, Florida, and Alabama

I have two different partners with whom I'm actively buying deals. The first is an active partnership where we split everything (profits and costs) 50/50 and separate the partnership duties based on our strengths. We invest in both short- and long-term rentals.

My second partnership is new, but I've already bought two houses with this partner in the last four months, and we have ambitions to continue building our business. This is an arrangement where my partner brings all the money to the deal, and I do all the work. If we leave any money in after the refinance (these are BRRRR deals), my partner will hold that money in the property. This partnership is really going to help me scale because I'm able to deploy my partner's capital and use my strengths in finding deals and managing rehabs to our mutual advantage.

CONCLUSION

It is clear that forming partnerships in the real estate industry can bring significant benefits. By forming partnerships, investors can access more cash, acquire bigger deals, and achieve higher profits. Additionally, having a partner with complementary skills, expertise, and networks can help investors to achieve their real estate investment goals. However, it is important to choose the right partner carefully to maximize the benefits of the partnership. Finding the right real estate partner requires careful consideration and a strategic approach.

The Summary

As an investor you should be identifying your investment goals and needs. This should already be something you have implemented in your business. If you don't know, now is the time to do that. Be clear about what you want to achieve through the partnership, your investment strategy, and the type of properties you want to invest in. Don't wait for a potential partner to come to you; get out there and source some partners! Attend real estate conferences and events, join local real estate clubs, and connect with other investors to build relationships and expand your network. Look for investors with complementary skills and experience who share similar goals and values. As a last warning, before entering into a partnership, conduct a thorough background check, review their track record, and make sure that their financial standing is sound. Once it's clear you want to partner with someone, don't forget to put it in writing. Work with a lawyer to draft a detailed partnership agreement that outlines each partner's responsibilities, ownership structure, and exit strategy. Lastly, maintain open and honest communication with your partner throughout the partnership, and work collaboratively to achieve your investment goals.

The Pyramid

Lastly, before you head on to read your next book, let's review the importance of the Partnership Pyramid. The Partnership Pyramid is a framework for understanding the important components of a real estate partnership. The first layer is Goals, which involves ensuring both partners are aligned and share the same vision for the partnership. The second layer is Structure, which refers to each partner's specific roles, responsibilities, and ownership terms. The final layer is Communication, which is crucial for the success of any relationship and involves both speaking and active listening. By building each layer of the Partnership Pyramid, partners can establish a strong foundation for a successful working relationship. As you continue to build out your partnership, keep this framework in mind. Get one of those cheesy posters to hang on your wall in your office to remind you of what it takes to keep your partnership rock-solid.

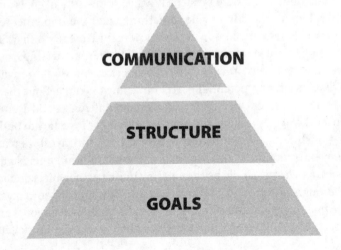

The Send-Off

The partnership journey can be a mixed bag of emotions, but being prepared and properly planning your partnership can take your investing to the next level. We commend you for taking the time to read this book—your partnership is already one step ahead of most people's. We wish you the best in your success. Now, go lock up some deals with your partner!

ACKNOWLEDGMENTS

We never knew our lives would lead to having the opportunity to share our real estate investing knowledge with all of you. As we look back on the process of bringing this book to life, we are filled with gratitude for those who have been with us every step of the way. To our family and friends, thank you for your unwavering love and support and for being a constant source of inspiration. Our current business partners, Sara, Omid, Evan, Joe, and Daryl, have educated us, been patient with us, and brought so many changes to our lives. We could never have written a how-to book without our experiences, good and bad, with them. Thank you for taking this roller coaster of trial and error to get where we are today as partners.

To the BiggerPockets Publishing Team, thank you for your guidance and expertise and for helping shape this book into its final form. Savannah Wood, Katie Miller, and Kaylee Walterbach brought this book to life! Thank you to Peri Eryigit for sharing this book with the world! We are grateful to the editors and designers who made this book look as appealing as the content inside it: Thank you to Wendy Dunning, Haley Montgomery, Melissa Brandzel, Hayden Seder, and Janice Bryant.

For about six months our podcast producers had to put up with us double-booking publishing meetings and podcast recordings. Thank you to the *Real Estate Rookie* producers, Eric Knutson and Daniel Zarate, for always putting up with us and giving us a voice.

Finally, to the Real Estate Rookie Rockstars who pour their hearts into sharing Real Estate Investing with everyone around them: You are changing lives by just introducing the idea of a real estate strategy, planting that seed to start them on their journey.

More from
BiggerPockets Publishing

If you enjoyed this book, we hope you'll take a moment to check out some of the other great material BiggerPockets offers. Whether you crave freedom or stability, a backup plan, or passive income, **BiggerPockets** empowers you to live life on your own terms through real estate investing.

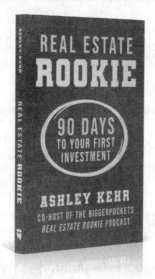

Real Estate Rookie

At 26 years old, Ashley Kehr was deep in debt and working at a career she no longer loved. Now, less than a decade later, she manages a portfolio of more than thirty properties and has achieved complete financial freedom. With this book, you'll be able to transform even faster—in fact, within ninety days you could already own your first property. Real estate investing can seem impossible when you're a rookie, and your first investment will no doubt be the hardest. Ashley's tried-and-true plan will fast-track your growth from real estate rookie to real estate rockstar.

More from
BiggerPockets Publishing

If you enjoyed this book, we hope you'll take a moment to check out some of the other great material BiggerPockets offers. Whether you crave freedom or stability, a backup plan, or passive income, **BiggerPockets** empowers you to live life on your own terms through real estate investing.

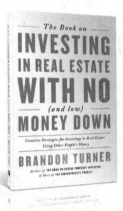

The Book on Investing in Real Estate with No (and Low) Money Down

Is your lack of cash holding you back from your real estate dreams? Discover the creative real estate financing techniques that savvy investors are using to do more deals, more often. Longtime cohost of *The BiggerPockets Podcast*, Brandon Turner, dives into multiple financing methods that professional investors use to tap into current real estate markets. Not only will you be able to navigate the world of creative real estate finance, you'll get more mileage out of any real estate investment strategy!

The Book on Tax Strategies for the Savvy Real Estate Investor

Taxes! Boring and irritating, right? Perhaps. But if you want to succeed in real estate, your tax strategy will play a huge role in how fast you grow. A great tax strategy can save you thousands of dollars a year. A bad strategy could land you in legal trouble. With *The Book on Tax Strategies for the Savvy Real Estate Investor*, you'll find ways to deduct more, invest smarter, and pay far less to the IRS!

172

Find the **information**, **inspiration**, and **tools** you need to dive right into the world of real estate investing with confidence.

 Sign up today—it's free! Visit **www.BiggerPockets.com**

 Find our books at **www.BiggerPockets.com/store**

First-Time Home Buyer: The Complete Playbook to Avoiding Rookie Mistakes

Everything you need to buy your first home, from initial decisions all the way to the closing table! Scott Trench and Mindy Jensen of the *BiggerPockets Money Podcast* have been buying and selling houses for a collective thirty years. In this book, they'll give you a comprehensive overview of the home-buying process so you can consider all of your options and avoid pitfalls while jumping into the big, bad role of homeowner.

Real Estate by the Numbers: A Complete Reference Guide to Deal Analysis

Whether you're looking to purchase your first rental property, scale a portfolio, or evaluate massive syndication deals, every great real estate deal comes down to a few key metrics. From cash flow to compound interest, *Real Estate by the Numbers* makes it easy for anyone to master the concepts that form the foundation of real estate investing. J Scott—best-selling author of four business books—and Dave Meyer—VP of Analytics at BiggerPockets—combine their data-driven investing experience to teach you everything you need to analyze deals, track your progress, and think like a professional investor.

Looking for more?
Join the BiggerPockets Community

BiggerPockets brings together education, tools, and a community of more than 2+ million like-minded members—all in one place. Learn about investment strategies, analyze properties, connect with investor-friendly agents, and more.

Go to **biggerpockets.com** to learn more!

 Listen to a **BiggerPockets Podcast**

 Watch **BiggerPockets on YouTube**

 Join the **Community Forum**

 Learn more on **the Blog**

 Read more **BiggerPockets Books**

 Learn about our **Real Estate Investing Bootcamps**

 Connect with an **Investor-Friendly Real Estate Agent**

 Go Pro! Start, scale, and manage your portfolio with your **Pro Membership**

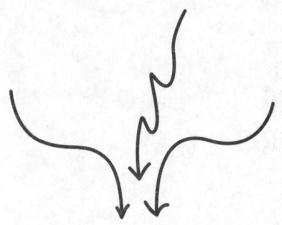

Follow us on social media!

Sign up for a Pro account
and take **20 PERCENT OFF**
with code **BOOKS20**.